P9-DMO-049

Tim Simond

DIVE IN STYLE

With 743 color illustrations

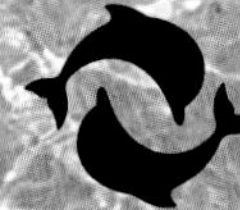
Thames & Hudson

PAGE 1, TOP LEFT AND RIGHT
Huvafen Fushi, Maldives, the sister hotel to Dhoni Mighili

PAGE 1, BOTTOM LEFT
Soneva Gili resort, Maldives

PAGE 1, BOTTOM RIGHT
The Seychelles

PAGES 2–3
The Great Barrier Reef, Australia

For Bill, who threw us in at the deep end and unwittingly started us on this odyssey.

First published in 2006 in hardcover in the United States of America by Thames & Hudson Inc., 500 Fifth Avenue, New York, New York 10110

thamesandhudsonusa.com

Library of Congress Catalog Card Number 2005907158

ISBN-13: 978-0-500-51292-0
ISBN-10: 0-500-51292-2

Printed and bound in China

contents

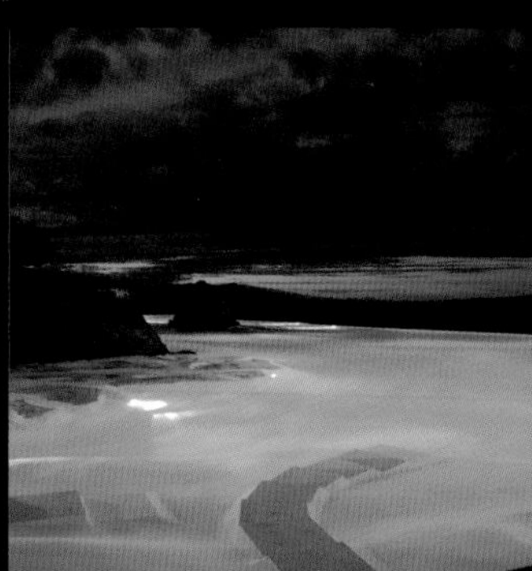

introduction

'Staying on top of the water is like standing outside the circus tent.' With two-thirds of our planet covered in water, there's truth in this quip. Recreational diving is a new sport, really only available since the 1960s, and then only for the adventurous. Indeed, even fifteen years ago, the image was of a small band of hardcore enthusiasts clad in unflattering neoprene, living in barrack-like accommodation and engaged in what was seen as an extreme and uncomfortable sport. Today diving has changed beyond recognition, with 15 million enthusiasts worldwide and nearly a million newcomers each year. It has also moved upmarket.

This book was driven by the observation that while the appeal of diving had spread to all levels of society, information on the subject had not. If you wanted a luxury holiday with great diving, where you could dive in small groups or learn without being part of a huge class but your family wanted other distractions, would it be easy to find the right place to go? Unfortunately not. There were 'Dive Hotels', but no obvious luxury or stylish hotels with diving. It was just as hard to find out about snorkelling.

But now things are different. After over a hundred flights and two years of research, we've come up with twenty-two hotels and four boats, all of which fulfil these criteria. Whether you dive, snorkel, or just want to chill, any of these will make a fantastic holiday.

Mankind's devastating effect on the planet has been most strongly felt in the world's oceans. Reefs have been destroyed, poisoned and dynamited, and are now threatened by global warming, the marine life decimated. The further away from development, the healthier the state of the marine environment tends to be. Search however, and there are some fantastic 'compromises', twenty-six of which you will find here.

INTRODUCTION

The featured hotels are spread all over the world, all in temperate waters, and stretch from the Mediterranean to the Maldives. Obviously, you cannot compare the diving experience over such a diverse spread, but every one in its own way is the best that each area of the world has to offer and they all have their own unique appeal. Whittled down from a list of over 125 candidates, the final choices were all based on merit only, and none of them paid to be included.

A further point taken into account was families. 'Dive Hotels' tend to cater just for divers. It may be that you are the only diver in the family, but while you enjoy yourself, what does the rest of your family do? None of these hotels is a dedicated dive resort; they are all just wonderful resorts in their own right, which cater for divers much as they cater for tennis or any other sport, and this makes them very different. Consequently, we have looked at their restaurants, spas, excursions, facilities and especially snorkelling in order to provide a general view of the resort, not just a diver's perspective. This is not just a dive book; you could happily holiday at any of these resorts without even thinking of diving and still have an amazing time.

We have tried to show these hotels in a realistic light, including only what you will really see. No models, no sets, no carefully arranged food or champagne picnics; in fact we were just like any other holidaymakers, taking photographs with no special treatment. Every underwater photograph was taken during our short stay, so if we saw something, there is a good chance that you will too – there has been no rush to a photo library for a shot of a rare pygmy seahorse or scalloped hammerhead, even though we could well have seen those species and you might yet. The rule is that if we did not see it, then it's simply not in the book. The overall aim was simply to show what we saw, both on land and underwater.

We hope you enjoy this book, and should you require any further information about any of these resorts, have any useful tips from your own trips, or believe that we have missed out a worthy contender, please visit our website – www.diveinstyle.com – and give us your feedback.

UNDERWATER PHOTOGRAPHY

This is a very difficult art to master, but thanks to digital cameras with effectively limitless film, it has never been easier to start. Today, many manufacturers such as Olympus, Sony and Canon all make suitable inexpensive underwater housings. The easiest and most fun way to start is with a small digital camera that you can slip into your BC. However it does have serious limitations, the prime one being light as all colour is effectively lost when you are only thirty feet underwater and flash is needed to bring it out. While all digital cameras have a built-in flash, their power is limited, so if you want better images, your first addition should be a separate flashgun. Unfortunately that means bulk and you will no longer be able to slip it into your BC, and this in turn means that you need to be a more accomplished diver if you are to avoid damaging the reefs.

In order to do this, you will need excellent buoyancy and spatial awareness. Consequently, these are skills you should have mastered to some degree before you impose yourself on the reefs. Bear in mind that you should never touch live reef, and you will begin to understand the difficulty of hovering inches over a bed of sea urchins while trying for that elusive toadfish shot.

There is so much that goes into this hobby that I could do no better than refer you to experts. Ocean Optics of London (www.oceanoptics.co.uk) will give you totally unbiased advice, and while I am the first to look for a discount, this was one time I was happy to pay sticker price; they know their business and will give honest advice, even to the extent of losing themselves a sale.

australia

Visible from space and stretching halfway up the eastern coast of Australia, the Great Barrier Reef is home to an incredible diversity of marine life. From the cooler waters in the south to the more temperate waters in the north, you'll find some fifteen hundred species of fish alone, as well as over four hundred kinds of coral.

This colossus of a barrier reef has not been immune to the effects of El Niño and global warming, but somehow the north seems to have escaped – most notably around Ribbon Reef 10, a few miles from Lizard Island. Remote enough for you to escape the hordes of day trippers, Lizard Island gives you access to the kind of diving that is normally the exclusive preserve of live-aboards.

A three-hour flight from Sydney takes you to Cairns, the jumping-off spot for Lizard Island. While Cairns itself is nothing special, it's worth exploring the coast running north towards Cape Tribulation, which is unique for having more than two million acres of rainforest running directly into the ocean.

While the Great Barrier Reef is protected as a World Heritage site, Lizard Island also enjoys the status of a marine park. It seems almost contradictory for such a pristine natural environment to be paired with a world-class hotel, yet that's exactly what makes this the perfect place to discover the world's largest reef system.

Gazing down from the plane, it's easy enough to see why these are called the Ribbon Reefs: the breaking surf forms a series of wavy white lines against the deep turquoise ocean. The individual reefs are identified not with names but numbers: Ribbon Reef 1 is next door to Ribbon Reef 2, and so on. This no-nonsense approach is typically Australian: it's simple but it works.

lizard island

HOTEL lizard island lodge

Located close to Ribbon Reef 10, Lizard Island hosts the northernmost island resort on the Great Barrier Reef, as well as a marine research station and a large number of the monitor lizards from which it takes its name. Despite being so close to the tropics, this 2,500-acre pocket of land is somewhat barren due to the constant wind and lack of rainfall, but don't let that put you off: its shores are lined with twenty-four white-sand beaches, which alone are worth the trip. Lizard Island Lodge occupies the most beautiful and protected of these. Originally built in 1975 and now part of the exclusive Voyages group, this exclusive retreat combines the very best in accommodation with access to some truly spectacular diving.

A three-minute ride from the island's simple airstrip delivers you to the hotel's discreet single-storey lodge, a wide, wooden-floored expanse with deep wicker sofas and timber chairs that sets the tone of laid-back luxury. Radiating out like wings on either side of the lodge are the rooms, usually arranged in pairs, which feature bright, modern Australian-style decor. All open directly onto shady private terraces; some offer a daybed, while others provide a hammock. Your experience will depend on where you stay. The Sunset Villas, built on the gently sloping hillside above Sunset Beach, are set in natural bush, while the Anchor Bay Suites and Rooms, each

at a glance

Airport	Cairns via Sydney
Airlines	Qantas or British Airways, then Macair to Lizard Island (baggage weight limit 20kg)
Transfer time	55 mins by plane
Rooms	40 (all air-conditioned)
Staff ratio	1+
Activities	Walks, glass-bottom boat tours, research station visits, fishing, catamarans, dinghies, beach picnics, spa, gym, swimming pool, tennis, glass-bottom paddle skis, snorkel lessons
Services	Internet, television, DVD and CD player in Departure Lounge
Children	12+
Power type	3-pin angled flat
Currency	Australian dollar
GMT	+10
Telephone	+61 7 40431999
Website	www.lizardisland.com.au
Booking	www.diveinstyle.com

with their own white-sand track leading to the main beach, are fronted by a rolling green lawn, palms, pine trees and sea roses. The former give a sense of being in the Australian bush; the latter have the feel of a beach holiday. For the best of both worlds, the lofty Pavilion or 'Pavy' delivers, and comes complete with your own private pool.

The resort's impact on the island's environment is minimal; nature has been tamed, but there are no manicured flowerbeds. Instead, you'll come across some much more interesting features such as the seemingly permanently occupied sunbird's nest that hangs adjacent to the bar, or the monitor lizards drinking from your giant clam footbath... it's here that the resort just morphs into nature.

As expected, the food represents the best of Australian fusion cooking. With the exception of private beachside picnics, meals are served in in the lodge's semi-circular dining pavilion overlooking the beach and the ocean beyond. There are no windows or walls to separate you from the great outdoors – this is alfresco, Aussie-style.

While you're here, you can do as much or as little as you like. At your disposal is a fleet of fully prepared motorized dinghies that will take you, along with a serious picnic hamper, to any beach you desire. You can also walk to remote bays, trek up to Cook's Point for the view or take a glass-bottom boat tour. If you prefer stay put, there are plenty of options for relaxing. The freshwater swimming pool is great for chilling out, or you can spoil yourself with treatments based on marine ingredients at the Azure Spa.

When it's time to go, there's the Guest Departure Lounge, which lets you enjoy yourself up until the last minute. Room check-out is in the late morning, but most flights leave in the afternoon; here you can take advantage of showers, bathrooms and suitcase storage. It's a final touch of hospitality that makes for a sweet end to your stay at Lizard Island – a very special bolthole with an Antipodean flavour, where 'no worries' means just that.

Located opposite the fleet of bobbing yellow dinghies at the western end of the hotel's beach, the Beach Club features a classroom, storage rooms, hanging racks and even a small dive shop. A full range of top-class gear is available, but if you bring your own, one of the friendly team will collect it from your room and look after it throughout your stay.

DIVE CENTER

The boat is normally the comfortable, beamy 53ft MV Serranidae, which provides plenty of dry cover and an upper sun deck; if things get really busy a 42ft fishing boat can also be pressed into service.

Every other day there are full-day excursions to outer reef dive sites, including the world-famous Cod Hole. On other days half-day excursions to closer reef systems are offered. When booking, just check that your dates don't coincide with the very rare bad tides or else you might not be able to dive.

On arrival at the dive sites, an army of staff swing into a ballet of action to moor the boat. Access is by a giant stride off a sea-level platform, and returning to the boat couldn't be easier: your gear is lifted off your back and the bottle changed, leaving you free to enjoy the amazing lunch. For divers or snorkellers, this trip is a must.

It's a shame that no courses are offered at such a flawless dive operation, but it's still possible to do your open-water certification dives. Let them know in advance if you are doing your pool work elsewhere so they can tell you what documents to bring; their rules are strict, but like everything else in this set-up, safety is at the forefront of their minds.

at a glance

Boats	53ft (dry, covered)
Group size	6
Instructors	8+
Languages	English
Courses	Resort and refresher courses; open-water qualification dives, subject to conditions
Children	14+
Other	Computer hire, superb food and drinks, gear prep and wash down, private charters, dive shop

Exploring the Great Barrier Reef is a truly memorable experience, especially in these still relatively untouched northern waters. The size, variety and sheer quantity of corals and sea life have to be seen to be believed, and you never know what you might encounter on each dive – there always seems to be something different. For non-divers, the snorkelling is superb; you can float over the reefs' sun-dappled shallows and not miss a thing.

DIVING

Cod Hole is the best-known dive site, renowned for its friendly or perhaps simply greedy giant potato cod. The dive begins with controlled feeding at roughly 30ft: you kneel on the sea floor while 80lb-plus cod swim around you, waiting for lunch to be shared out by your guide. In exchange for the meal, they happily put up with being gently stroked. For snorkellers, they lure the cod up to you.

While this is fun, it's worth splitting off as soon as you can to explore the outer reef wall, which drops down to roughly 70ft before reaching the main drop-off. An easy dive, it is home to clownfish, Napoleon wrasse, bumphead parrotfish, green moray, lionfish... the list goes on. But what really sets this site apart is the condition and sheer quantity of the brilliant multicoloured corals, including truly wonderful blue and turquoise staghorns.

New Reef is a gentle, shallow dive, with acres of perfect staghorn and cabbage corals. Its aquarium-like beauty is just as good for snorkelling: you can spend hours in just a few feet of water, picking over the coral and spotting anything from tiny flatworms to what must be some of the world's most enormous clams, at around 4ft long. There's also Dynamite Pass, which can be either an easy dive or, if the current is flowing, a drift dive. Along with all the usual

at a glance

Local sites	2, plus endless sites on Great Barrier Reef (weather dependent)
Level	Easy
Visibility	100ft on outer reef; 50ft on inner reef
Must-dives	Cod Hole, Dynamite Pass, No Name Reef
Snorkelling	Excellent on house reef, superb from dive boat
Wetsuits	5mm (3mm in summer)
Coral	Pristine
Marine life	Giant clams, giant potato cod, Napoleon wrasse, bumphead parrotfish, humpback and minke whale, manta ray, shark, green moray, lionfish, clownfish
Other	Hyperbaric chamber at Townsville (2 hrs), day trips to barrier reef and inner reef on alternate days, marine park

TOP LEFT
You can snorkel among dozens of giant clams, some over a hundred years old, at Mrs Watson's Clam Garden. A marine biologist will be your guide.

RIGHT, ABOVE AND BELOW
The sheer quantity, quality and variety of coral on the Great Barrier Reef is simply breathtaking.

suspects, you are almost guaranteed to come across an inquisitive (and hungry) Napoleon wrasse, as well as sleeping white-tip reef sharks. With reasonable air consumption, you can expect to spend well over an hour underwater on all these dives, so at least a 5mm wetsuit is a must.

Closer to home, North Direction Island (so called thanks to the straightforward Aussie naming system) and Magillivrays Reef tend to offer less visibility but wonderful diving. The fringe reef surrounding the former is sheltered from prevailing winds so conditions are never really a problem. Ranging from about 15ft to 40ft in depth, the fine sandy floor is dotted with coral bommies, and you drift gently from one to another marvelling at the sea life, all of which are simply a cornershop version of the main event.

Returning from the day trip, a final treat awaits you: fish feeding, with a difference. Two 9ft-long nurse sharks come to the dive platform, behaving like a pair of puppies fighting for attention. You may also notice a dark brown shadow lurking in the water; this is Simon, a 500lb-plus, 8ft-long giant Queensland grouper. He'll surface when the smell of fish proves too much for him, but he's blisteringly fast, so don't look away.

LEFT
Snorkelling with green turtles off Casurina Beach, a great place for a picnic.

RIGHT
The Great Barrier Reef is where the real Nemo lives.

BELOW
An octopus looks unfazed as it poses for the camera.

LEFT
Giant potato cod are so large that they don't feel threatened by divers.

BELOW
A pair of large nurse shark regularly visit the dive platform, greedy for food and attention.

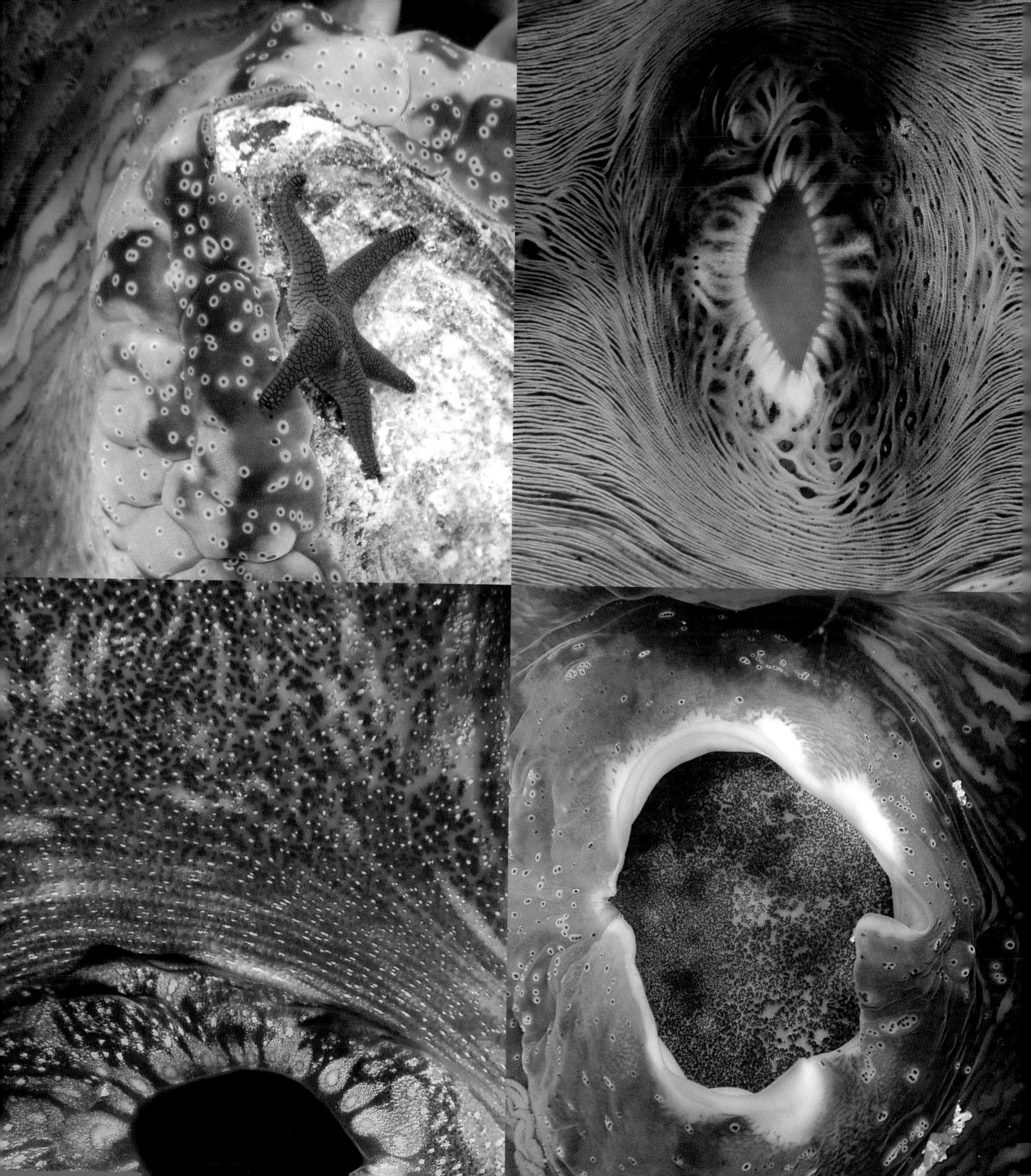

LEFT

The colours and details found on a giant clam would inspire any designer.

RIGHT

The beautiful Napoleon wrasse is under threat; in the Far East, it is prized for its Mick Jagger lips, which are considered a delicacy.

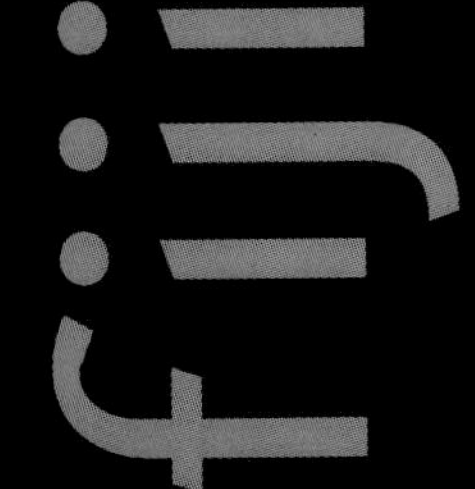

There was a time when the Fijians would rather eat you than greet you, but today the dreaded 'Cannibal Isles' are home to quite possibly the friendliest people on the planet. The country's blend of cultures is fascinating, and although there has been some well-publicized trouble between the indigenous Fijians and the Fijian Indians, this ethnic divide generally simmers in the background and should not be a deterrent to visiting.

Consisting of over 330 islands, Fiji has a population of only 850,000, 75 per cent of whom live on the main island of Viti Levu. This leaves at least 329 islands for the remaining few; many islands are deserted. Thus the pace of life drops once you make it to the outer islands, and 'crowd' becomes just another word in the dictionary.

Viti Levu is primarily given over to more mass-market hotels; you will almost certainly need to stay in one at some point due to airline schedules. The best option for overnighting is the Sheraton Royal Denarau, about a twenty-minute drive from the airport. While the mainland has its attractions, it's best not to spend too much time here: you will only discover the true beauty of this stunning archipelago by venturing further afield.

To the south of Viti Levu lies Vatulele, accessed by an easy twenty-five-minute journey by seaplane (flights depart direct from the airport). Seen from the air, you can fully appreciate the beauty of the main island, before soaring over the blue waters and honeycomb reefs to your private island retreat.

From the air Vatulele looks almost deserted. But this island and its perfect white-sand beach, anchored at both ends by volcanic headlands, are home to one of the finest resorts in Fiji. Built in 1991 by Emmy-award-winning producer Henry Crawford and business partner Martin Livingston, it has serious eco-credentials: it's one of the world's best examples of a hotel that not only coexists with its environment but also gives something back to it.

vatulele

HOTEL vatulele

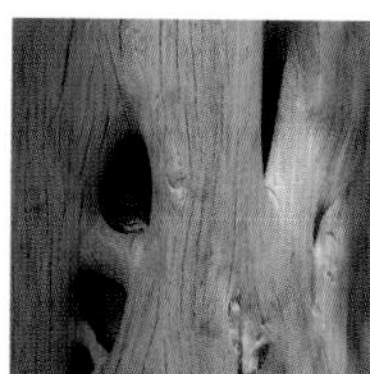

It's rare to come to an island where so many people are there specifically to celebrate something. But at Vatulele, honeymooners are everywhere, and there are always birthday celebrations and wedding anniversaries – all the guests seem to have chosen this place for a special occasion.

The magic begins on your arrival by seaplane: you land in a cloud of spray on a mirror-flat turquoise lagoon, and as your toes touch the powdery sand you hear the melodic sounds of singing and the timeless Fijian welcome of '*bula*'.

You reach your room or *bure* (pronounced 'boo-ray') via a shady walkway that winds its way around the mature indigenous trees. Despite being virtually invisible from the sea or air, all seventeen standard bures have sea views and direct beach access. While they share the same basic layout, some are adapted to incorporate natural features such as rocky outcrops or massive tree roots. The interior's architectural style is Santa Fe meets Fiji: ledges, niches and rounded concrete shapes are topped off (literally) with high ceilings, overhead fans, timber beams and intricate local rope work.

at a glance

Airport	Nadi
Airlines	Air New Zealand or Air Pacific
Transfer time	25 mins by seaplane
Rooms	19 (some air-conditioned)
Staff ratio	5+
Activities	Red prawn excursion, lighthouse walk, Kava village tour, island picnics, fishing, canoeing, tennis, in-room massage
Services	Room service
Children	12+
Power type	3-pin flat
Currency	Fijian dollar, US dollar
GMT	+12
Telephone	+679 6720300
Website	www.vatulele.com
Booking	www.diveinstyle.com

All rooms have fans, but if air-conditioning is a must for you, then look to either the Point or the Grand Bure. Above the beach on the headland, the Point is a spacious two-storey villa with unobstructed views of the reef and the main island of Viti Levu. Those lucky enough to stay here usually treat it as their island fortress; they rarely venture down to the resort as all their needs are catered for by a personal butler. The Grand Bure, on the beach but away from the core of the hotel, is also extremely private – a golf cart, driver and butler are all supplied. In design terms, it's less Fijian than the other bures, but it provides the kind of sybaritic luxury that's hard to resist.

Unlike most luxury hotels, Vatulele has an all-inclusive room rate. While the price may cause you to flinch at first, bear in mind that aside from massages and diving, it covers everything, and I do mean everything: you can sit back and relax knowing that however hard you try, however much champagne you drink, you'll be hard-pressed to create an extra bill. Communal dining is another hotel trend adopted here, but if the social mixing bowl isn't for you, you're free to go 'off piste': you can dine on the beach under the stars, lunch on another island, eat looking out to the ocean from a high pavilion, savour a meal in the wine cellar with a free choice of vintage... the list goes on.

There are plenty of activities, including a trip to see royal red prawns: a short boat ride and walk through a forest of orange-trunked palms takes you to a quiet pool at the base of granite cliffs, one of only thirty locations in Fiji where these crimson-shelled crustaceans still exist.

Vatulele is a peaceful, laid-back, toes-in-the-sand hideaway, totally at one with its surroundings. The beach is virtually always empty, so even when the resort is full you get the feeling of being on your own. You soon realize why people come to Vatulele for their most important moments: just being here is a reason to celebrate.

Vatulele is proud of the fact that all of its dive team are local. Situated just next door to the main bure, the small dive facility is owned and run as an adjunct to the hotel. With no fewer than four dive masters and one instructor, Vule, it is an excellent place to learn to dive, and many guests take either PADI or repeat resort courses here.

DIVE CENTER

Once you have chosen your gear, all of which is in excellent condition, you never have to lift a finger. Your ready-rigged equipment awaits you on the boat and disappears to be rinsed and dried after diving. The service is exceptional, and like virtually everything else in Fiji, it is carried out with smiling good humour.

A 16ft inflatable is equipped for diving, but most is done from the purpose-designed 24ft catamaran, the *Mai Nunu* ('Come Diving'). Boarding is from the beach and the boat is pulled right into the clear shallows so you hardly get your feet wet. The snorkelling off the beach is nothing particularly special, so either take a kayak out to the reef or join the dive boat.

With never more than four guests to a guide, and frequently just two, instructors can cater for divers of differing abilities; this is a painless way to dive, ideally suited to novice divers. There are also discounts for multiple dives, so it's well worth booking in advance.

Returning to the boat and hanging onto the ladder, I was startled to find something pulling at my fins. It was one of the dive team, head underwater, removing them for me. Such determination to look after you is typical here – this is the Vatulele way of doing things.

at a glance

Boats	24ft catamaran, 16ft rigid inflatable (dry, covered)
Group size	4
Instructors	1, plus 4 dive masters
Languages	English
Courses	All PADI
Children	12+
Other	Computer hire, drinks, gear prep and wash down, private charters

Fiji hosts some truly captivating diving, most of it remote and accessed only by live-aboards. El Niño and a few cyclones have done their best to damage the reefs, but fortunately nature has proven resilient. Vatulele offers gentle diving in perfect conditions, away from any crowds, and you can dive as shallow or deep as you like in clear, calm waters – there are virtually no currents.

ABOVE

The hard corals are well preserved, especially in the shallows; they're ideal for exploration during your safety stop.

DIVING

The reefs remain relatively unexplored and the dive team is constantly making new discoveries, particularly by the main pass on the windward side of Vatulele. The underwater topography is a series of peaks and valleys inhabited by hawksbill, green and loggerhead turtles, lionfish, spotted and green morays, and large stingrays. Fish life, though plentiful and usually oblivious to divers, can be somewhat cagey at sites where the locals still spear fish despite the resort's efforts to declare the area a marine park. But the great thing is that anything can appear on any given day, from inquisitive sailfish to killer whales and hammerhead sharks.

All the current sites are opposite the resort on the leeward side of the island, and you can pick and choose according to your ability. There are some excellent sheer walls that descend to 150ft and 200ft before reaching a plateau, then dropping into the abyss. Other sites rise as pinnacles from the depths; many of them have colourful caps at 20ft, ideal for a safety stop as you can still search the nooks for that hidden something.

Fiji is known for its trademark soft corals, and if you're after these then Tabletop Pinnacle is a must-dive. Dive to about 100ft and you come across beautifully coloured soft corals swaying in the

at a glance

Local sites	22
Level	Easy
Visibility	100ft (up to 150ft in winter)
Must-dives	Tabletop Pinnacle
Snorkelling	Good from dive boat or kayak
Wetsuits	3mm
Coral	Very good soft, recovering hard
Marine life	Sailfish, hammerhead shark, spotted eagle ray, white-tip reef shark, silver-tip reef shark, shovelnose ray, loggerhead turtle
Other	Night dives, wreck dive, hyperbaric chamber on Suva (25 mins)

RIGHT
Royal red prawns seen not on a dive, nor even a snorkel, but a wade.

BELOW RIGHT
Scouring the reefs here can turn up many a surprise, including stonefish, which are virtually invisible.

ABOVE
The best time to study the beautiful parrotfish is while they sleep at night in a protective cocoon of self-spun mucus.

RIGHT
A batfish is almost bound to check you out at Gisela's Arch.

gentle current. You'll need a flashlight to reveal their vividness, as all colour is effectively lost at this depth: black transforms into brilliant red, and white into fluorescent pink. Gisela's Arch, a swim-through patrolled by an inquisitive batfish, is just as rewarding.

The Wreck is a Japanese fishing boat sunk deliberately in 1997. The vessel now sits in 160ft of water and ironically is home to the giant tuna it once fished. With her decks at 130ft and her mast rising some 30ft above, she is encrusted with soft corals and fans. The wreck disappears in the gloom as you swim away to the nearby wall, where you'll find a profusion of life: pairs of butterflyfish, all manner of parrotfish, the occasional white-tip or grey reef shark, and schools of fusiliers and red bass are common sights. You'll also find multi-coloured clams, enormous spotted cowries and tiny nudibranchs.

For the more experienced and thrill-seeking advanced divers, on the 150ft shelf before the drop-off at Bird Island, there is reportedly a carpet of large shovelnose rays. Regardless of experience, anyone looking for comfortable diving at all levels will not be disappointed here.

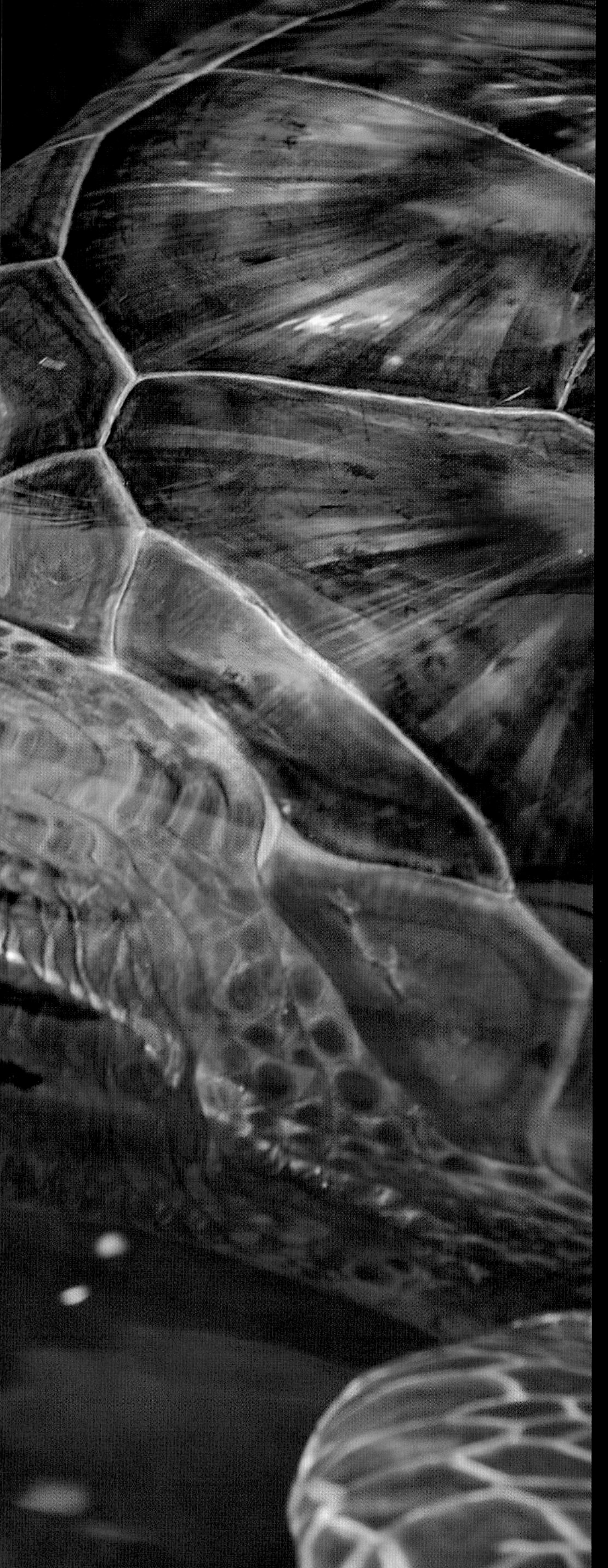

hawaii

Located right in the heart of the Pacific Ocean two thousand miles from the US mainland, Hawaii is the most remote island group on earth. Composed of six main islands – Maui, Lanai, Oahu, Kauai, Molokai and Hawaii (the largest) – it is so distant from any other land mass that a startling thirty per cent of its marine life can be found nowhere else on the planet. This makes for some truly special diving.

Your plane will deposit you on Oahu, most often associated with Pearl Harbor, Waikiki Beach and Pipeline, the surfing Mecca. With its beautiful interior and relatively unspoilt coastline, it merits your attention for a few days, especially if you are nursing a surfboard or a zeal for war history.

If time permits, it is worth staying in Maui for its two must-dives, Molokoni crater and Molokai; otherwise you can take a day trip from Lanai. A twenty-minute taxi ride from the town of Lahaina will bring you to the Maui Aquarium, where you will see everything from tiger shark to eagle ray, and with notice you can even dive with them.

Alternatively, fly straight off to the extraordinary island of Lanai to dive the pristine reefs or simply relax. An unspoilt gem surrounded by crystal waters, it rises from the ocean as brilliant red lava cliffs to a 3,400ft summit. If you're looking for Hawaii's best-kept secret, this is it.

Known for decades as the Pineapple Island, Lanai used to be home to sixteen thousand acres of the world's prickliest fruit; at one point it was its largest exporter. When the pineapple industry took a turn for the worse in the 1980s, Lanai took a turn for the better as the island reinvented itself as a world-class resort destination.

lanai

HOTEL manele bay

There are only two hotels of any size on Lanai, the Lodge at Koele and Manele Bay, both under the same stewardship as the privately owned island. While the former is inland and offers a fantastic golf-course, Manele Bay occupies the finest site on the island, chosen from fifty miles of pristine coastline. But the location's appeal doesn't stop there: spinner dolphins are such regular visitors to the hotel's bay that they were filmed here for the Discovery Channel.

Manele Bay's style is an unusual blend of Eastern and Hawaiian; it's eclectic but it works. Central to the resort are the high-ceilinged reception areas, which look out over terraces of thriving bougainvillea, the pool and the ocean beyond. A three-minute walk takes you to the quiet beach shared by the island's residents, but Lanai's population is so tiny that that it feels almost private.

Unlike most Hawaiian hotels, the rooms are arranged over two floors, and all enjoy wonderful views, whether they look out over the ocean or onto Manele Bay's lush Hawaiian gardens with their rushing waterfalls and pools full of koi carp. A major advantage of the oceanview rooms is that at the right time of year, you can lie on your bed and watch spinner dolphins at play, and humpback whales tail-slapping – this is totally effortless nature-watching.

at a glance

Airport	Lanai via Honolulu
Airlines	American Airlines, Delta, Hawaiian, Continental, United Airlines
Transfer time	15 mins by bus
Rooms	236 (air-conditioned)
Staff ratio	1+
Activities	Hiking, 4 x 4 rental, golf, clay-shooting, tennis, gym, spa, swimming pool, horseriding, whale-watching
Services	Internet, telephone, television, room service
Children	All ages
Power type	2-pin flat
Currency	US dollar
GMT	-10
Telephone	+808 5653704
Website	www.islandoflanai.com
Booking	www.diveinstyle.com

The cuisine is international and of the highest quality. You can eat anywhere from poolside to the bar, and if you want to venture further afield, a regular shuttle service takes you up to the Golf Club overlooking the sea, or even higher to the Lodge at Koele.

Lanai is only a thirty-minute flight from Honolulu, but it's a trip back in time. This is Hawaii how it used to be: with a population of barely three thousand, it is still so tranquil that just two police cruisers and a jail with room for three seems like overkill. Manele Bay's pace reflects this: it is incredibly peaceful. Yet you will never be bored. You can hire a 4 x 4 and explore the miles of quiet trails and deserted beaches, or if you prefer to chill, you can indulge yourself with a massage in an open cabaña overlooking the ocean. The resort is also very child-friendly, so if you want some time alone there are programmes to keep the kids busy.

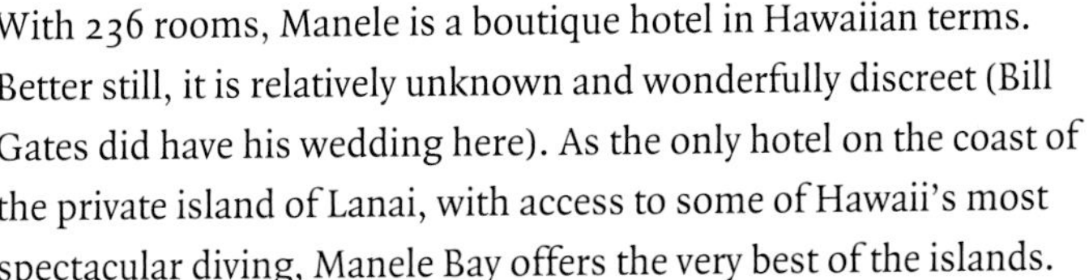

With 236 rooms, Manele is a boutique hotel in Hawaiian terms. Better still, it is relatively unknown and wonderfully discreet (Bill Gates did have his wedding here). As the only hotel on the coast of the private island of Lanai, with access to some of Hawaii's most spectacular diving, Manele Bay offers the very best of the islands.

The dive center on Lanai is run by Trilogy Excursions, located in Lahaina Harbor and just a three-minute bus ride from Manele Bay. A well-respected Maui-based operator, it handles virtually all watersports activities on the island, arranging not just diving, but also humpback whale tours and other water-based excursions.

DIVE CENTER

The center is small and has excellent diving equipment, but at present it offers only a limited variety of dives for exploring the area around Lanai. The diving here deserves more – much more – than this. However, the situation is bound to change as the secret of Lanai gets out.

A change of management at Manele Bay should help: the Four Seasons group are the hotel's new managers, and they realize what a natural goldmine they are sitting on – they are well experienced in catering to the demand for diving from high-end travellers. Nonetheless, to be safe, make sure the hotel knows you are coming to dive when you book, and it's even worth telling them when you want to dive during your stay.

If Trilogy is unable to fulfil your dreams, help is at hand from Extended Horizons, a small but top-rate Maui-based group that dives Lanai every day. For a small supplement (a local tax) they will pick you up at Lahaina Harbor, at the same place as Trilogy. They also run a year-round shore-based manta dive on Maui, which offers a good excuse to see the island and its aquarium, and makes for a great day trip from Lanai.

at a glance

Boats	32ft rigid inflatable (wet, covered)
Group size	6
Instructors	1+
Languages	English
Courses	All PADI
Children	12+
Other	Drinks, gear wash down, private charters, dive shop, underwater scooters
Website	www.sailtrilogy.com www.scubadivemaui.com

Voted one of the ten best dive destinations in the world by *Scuba Diving* and *Skin Diver* magazines, Lanai is second only to the Maui-based dives of Molokoni crater and Molokai. Some consider it even better: many Maui-based diving operators journey to Lanai in preference to their home sites. The island is an extinct volcano, making it a playground of swim-throughs and giant lava tubes or caves.

DIVING

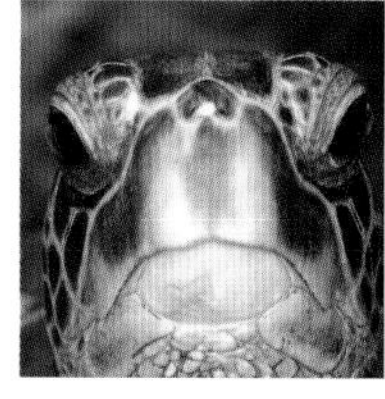

Lanai hosts world-renowned dives at First and Second Cathedrals, and they are not to be missed. Located just five hundred yards from the harbour at Lanai, these are 100ft-high tubes of hardened lava with streams of light filtering through their various 'stained-glass windows' or openings to the sea beyond. At the right time of day the light can fall dramatically onto an 'altar' or large boulder at First Cathedral (so called because you reach it first from Maui), adding to the atmosphere. Try and get there ahead of the rest of your group as the fine silt on the floor is all too easily stirred up by less experienced divers; this can spoil the perfect clarity, and with it the whole effect.

A number of dive sites play host to a phenomenon that appears to be particular to Hawaii: green turtle 'cleaning stations'. At both Turtle Haven and Oscar's Reef you can watch the turtles hover with their necks extended and fins held vertically, while grazing tang fish pick them clean. Interestingly, unlike many Maui turtles which carry tumours, Lanai turtles seem clear of them, possibly due to having less interaction with man or it may just be the slower pace of life.

One site, the Lighthouse, is home to several big white-tip shark, while another, Wash Rock, hosts rare creatures such as Tinker's butterflyfish. Normally deep-water dwellers, one or two have

at a glance

Local sites	30+
Level	Easy
Visibility	80–100ft
Must-dives	Cathedrals, Lighthouse
Snorkelling	Good on house reef and from dive boat
Wetsuits	3mm
Coral	Very good
Marine life	Humpback whale, spinner, spotted and bottlenose dolphin, moray eel (14 species), Tinker's butterflyfish, monk seal, Hawaiian lionfish, frogfish, white-tip reef shark, hammerhead shark, tiger shark, nudibranch, eagle ray, green turtle, flame wrasse
Other	Night dives, hyperbaric chamber on Oahu (1 hr)

TOP LEFT
Consider making a day trip to Maui to be virtually guaranteed close manta encounters.

RIGHT
When baby reindeer wrasse grow up, they look like a completely different species – rather like humans do.

taken up residence in shallower waters. The visibility is perfect and the hard corals seem to have been untouched by El Niño, but don't forget to look out into the big blue for hammerhead, tiger shark, eagle ray and even the rare Hawaiian monk seal. During the humpback season your dive will be accompanied by the beautifully haunting sound of whale song.

The clear water around Lanai and the untouched nature of its sites are unmatched even at Molokai and Molokoni, cementing this as one of the best diving spots in Hawaii, and therefore the USA. Because Lanai's sites are so close to Manele Bay – you can see the Cathedrals from your bed – it's easy to arrange to dive them when no one else is around, making your experience all the more special.

RIGHT
The rare Tinker's butterflyfish, usually dwelling in deeper waters, has decided to make itself more accessible to Lanai's divers.

LEFT
The cute Hawaiian white-spotted toby sports emerald-green eyes.

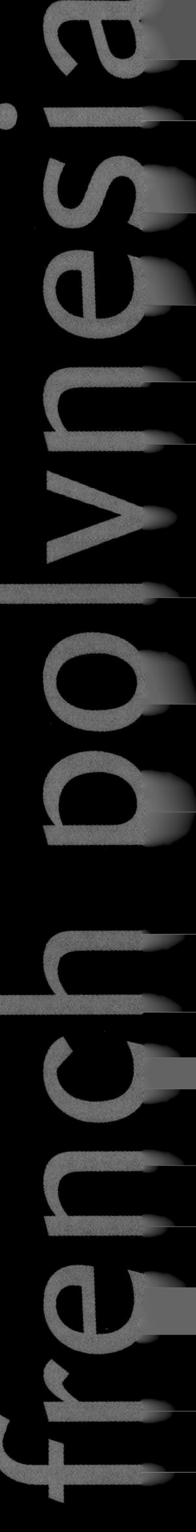

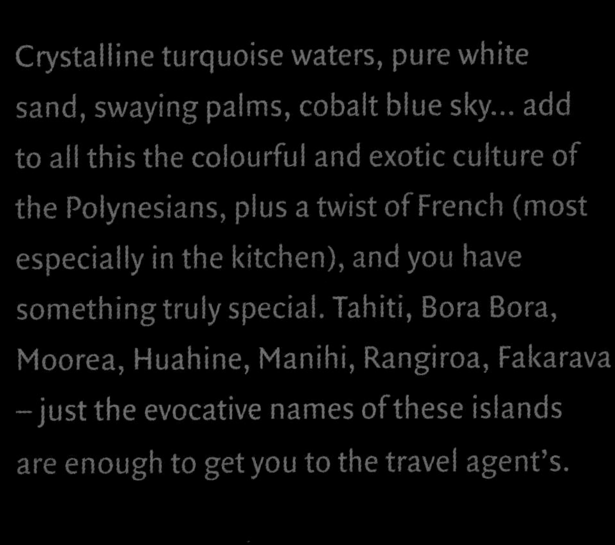

Crystalline turquoise waters, pure white sand, swaying palms, cobalt blue sky... add to all this the colourful and exotic culture of the Polynesians, plus a twist of French (most especially in the kitchen), and you have something truly special. Tahiti, Bora Bora, Moorea, Huahine, Manihi, Rangiroa, Fakarava – just the evocative names of these islands are enough to get you to the travel agent's.

There is, however, one drawback: you won't find Papeete listed alongside Tokyo and London as one of the world's most expensive cities – but it should be. That aside, once you have made the pilgrimage to this remote part of the world, it is well worth taking in three or even four islands. Flight schedules mean you normally have to spend a night in Papeete at the beginning and end of your trip. But unless you're a Gauguin fanatic or plan to explore the beautiful interior, you will probably want to give Tahiti herself a miss as – surprisingly – this is not really a beach destination since there is no natural white sand here.

Spread over an area nine times the size of their mother country, the islands that make up French Polynesia are composed primarily, although not exclusively, of the Society Islands and the Tuamotus. Linked by Air Tahiti Nui's domestic arm, the former are extraordinarily beautiful volcanic islands with lofty peaks clad in verdant jungle; the latter, low-lying coral atolls strung out like pearls (and also producing them). These island groups are separated by only a few hundred miles, but it might as well be a few thousand, so different is the experience

Hotel Bora Bora was the first hotel to open on this magically beautiful island after US forces abandoned their base here at the end of the Second World War. Naturally enough it claimed the prime spot, Matira Point, the only mainland site with its own white sand beach and a totally unobstructed, private view over the crystalline waters of the lagoon.

bora bora

HOTEL **hotel bora bora**

Bora Bora is still a challenger for the title of most beautiful island in the world. It centres upon a dormant volcanic peak, the flat-topped Mount Otemanu, which is slowly, very slowly, subsiding into the turquoise waters below. The flight from Tahiti takes forty-five minutes and deposits you at the small idyllic airport built on one of the tiny *motus* or islands that surround Bora Bora; the approach allows you to gaze back over the beauty of your destination. Even before you claim your bags, you will have been spotted by one of the hotel team, and a small private water taxi will take you the twenty minutes across the calm lagoon to the hotel. Pulling up to the dock, we interrupted a cruising shark and two manta ray enjoying their evening plankton meal – a foretaste of what awaited us underwater.

You may have heard reports of the ruin of Bora Bora. And to a degree it's true, development here has gone fairly berserk. But do not be put off – it's all relative. Hotel Bora Bora is a bit of a Grande Dame of the islands. Some would argue she needs a nip and a tuck, but despite her years she is still a class act and knows it, offering a style and setting that these new, sometimes flashy, pretenders simply cannot match. And thanks to the hotel's position in almost botanical gardens, you are blissfully unaware here of how the rest of the island has changed. The experience remains calm, private and serene.

at a glance

Airport	Bora Bora via Papeete
Airlines	Air New Zealand, Air Tahiti Nui, Qantas, Air France
Transfer time	20 mins by boat
Rooms	54 (all air-conditioned)
Staff ratio	3
Activities	Island tour, fishing, sailing, aqua safari, desert island picnics, helicopter tours, tennis, in-room massage
Services	Internet, telephone, television (in Activities Faré), CD player, room service, mobile phones
Children	All ages
Power type	2-pin round, 2-pin flat
Currency	French Pacific franc, US dollar
GMT	-10
Telephone	+689 604460
Website	www.amanresorts.com
Booking	www.diveinstyle.com

POFAI BEACH
BAR-RESTAURANT

Opened in 1961, the hotel originally had some ninety rooms, but – rather against the trend – this has since been reduced to just fifty-four. Legend has it that it was here, at Hotel Bora Bora, that the idea of building hotel bedrooms on stilts over a lagoon was first conceived – a model since copied not just throughout French Polynesia but as far away as the Maldives. Overwater Bungalows aside, accommodation includes ordinary Bungalows (an excellent compromise), Pool Farés, with their own private plunge pool, and Beach Farés (*faré* is the Tahitian word for home). All rooms have private decks, and their cedar walls, oak floors, louvred blinds and shutters create a luxurious cocooning effect. A word of advice: if you are sensitive to noise then it is best to make clear when you book that you do not want a villa that backs on to the road behind.

Perched above the small but perfect white-sand beach is the main building, where historic photographs and old Polynesian paintings jostle for wall space. This houses the high-ceilinged, open-sided Matira restaurant, which affords one of the most agreeable dining experiences in the world. Used mostly for breakfast and dinner (at lunchtime you will most probably have your feet in the sand at Pofai Bar beneath), it is lit at night by guttering flares and candles; it is a very special place, served by an incredibly friendly and loyal staff.

Hotel Bora Bora was one of the world's great hotels even in the 1970s. Under the sensitive stewardship of the Aman group, it has only got better, and it is clear they are committed to cementing their position as the best hotel on the island, and probably the islands. It is a must-visit.

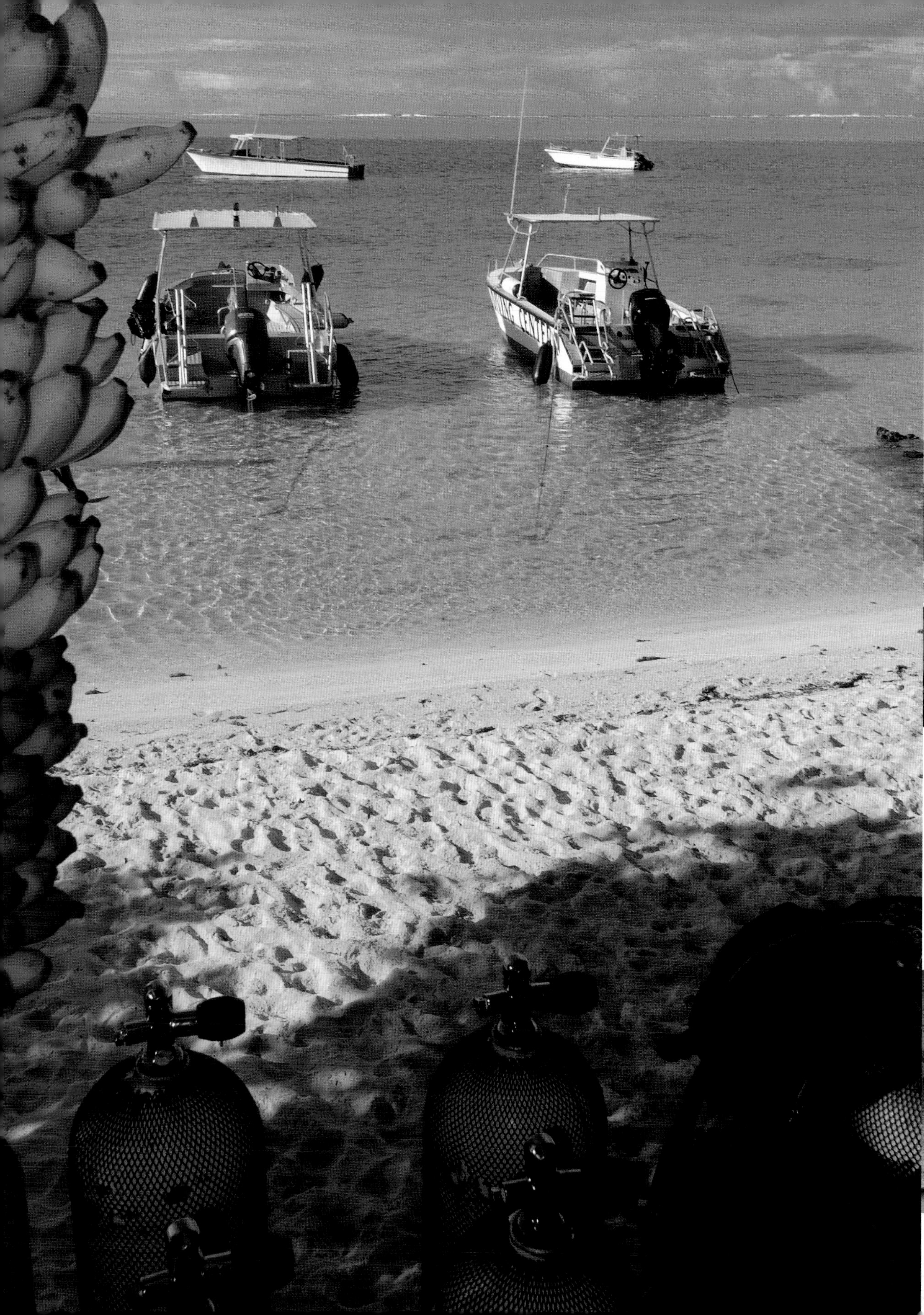

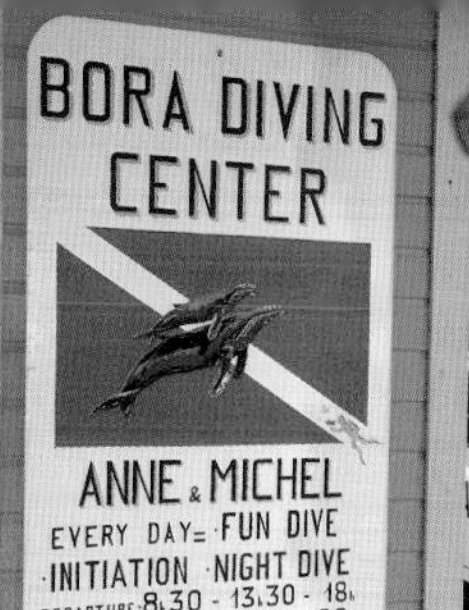

BORA DIVING CENTER
ANNE & MICHEL
EVERY DAY= ·FUN DIVE
·INITIATION ·NIGHT DIVE
DEPARTURE ·8h30 - 13h30 - 18h
RETURN - 10h30 - 15h30 - 20h

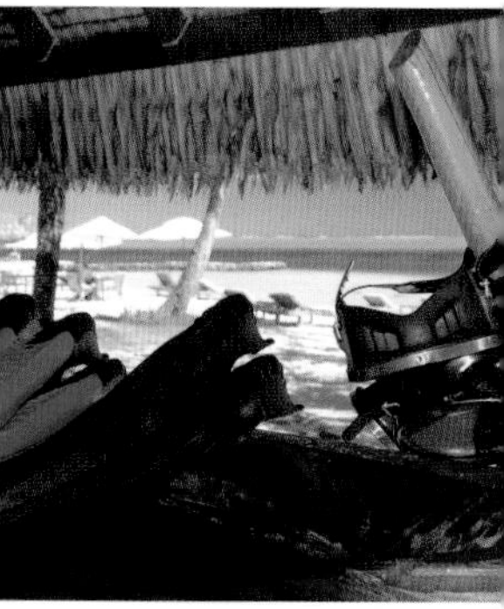

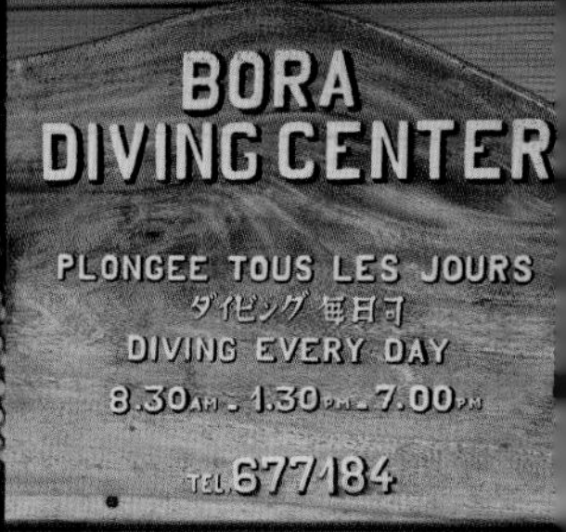
BORA
DIVING CENTER
PLONGEE TOUS LES JOURS
ダイビング 毎日可
DIVING EVERY DAY
8.30AM - 1.30PM - 7.00PM
TEL.677184

Situated beside the last beach bungalow, Bora Diving Center is owned not by Hotel Bora Bora but by Michel and Anne Condesse. However they treat the hotel – and therefore you – as their primary customer. Don't be put off by the apparent fleet of boats – this does not mean the diving is done on a large scale. In fact, it's quite the opposite.

DIVE CENTER

French Polynesia polices its diving carefully, and group dives are always kept small. What's more, the size of the Condesses' navy ensures that boats are seldom full, and the center will virtually always be able to arrange private charters.

The boats are functional but come with no frills, and while they do offer shade from the sun, there is no protection from the elements and very limited dry space – it's best to take a waterproof bag for towels and other dry items. There is also no provision for cameras, so be prepared to hold onto yours. Drinking water is supplied but not much else, so you'll need to fend for yourself if you want to snack between dives.

Pick-up from the hotel dock is militarily punctual, so don't be late. It's best to get into your wetsuit before boarding; there is a full range of gear available, and although somewhat old, it is regularly serviced. Unless you are setting the pace on your own private charter, things seem to happen at speed, especially on the two-tank dives, which have only a thirty-minute surface interval. While a more leisurely approach might be welcome, the center's efficiency does mean you have more time to enjoy the delights of the hotel.

at a glance

Boats	24ft (wet, covered)
Group size	5
Instructors	7
Languages	English, French
Courses	All PADI
Children	8+
Other	Drinks, gear prep and wash down, private charters, aqua safari (helmet diving, no tanks, no experience necessary)
Website	www.boradive.com

ABOVE
Clouds of butterflyfish congregate at Tapu and can literally envelop divers, especially when there is a lemon shark feeding.

It's quite simple: if you don't enjoy diving with shark and manta ray, Bora Bora is not for you; if you do, then this is world-class diving for all levels of experience, with more guaranteed pelagic action than virtually anywhere in the world. Add some of the best snorkelling on the planet, and you have a very special result. 'Awesome', for once, is no exaggeration.

DIVING

Tapu is probably the island's most famous site: as the only pass to the ocean, it is literally thick with life, most of which wants to be your friend. So good is the diving here that if you were allowed just one dive in Bora Bora, this should be it; non-divers can equally enjoy the sights from a yellow eight-seater submarine. Black-tip reef shark, Napoleon wrasse and lemon shark prowl the drop-off at about 100ft, while large moray eels, turtles and dense clouds of butterflyfish swim along the gently sloping walls of the massive plate and cabbage corals.

The trip to Muri Muri outside the reef can treat you to spinner dolphins or humpback whales even before you get wet. Then a backward roll drops you straight into a scene out of a James Bond movie, with tens of black-tip and grey reef sharks circling beneath you. It's best to descend quickly – you'll need little encouragement – to explore the sloping wall of coral, where there's a good chance of spotting hawksbill turtle before the reef descends into the abyss; afterwards drift with the current and you're back in the movie. While you hang onto the mooring line for your safety stop, look up to see all hell breaking loose; a tuna head thrown overboard creates a feeding frenzy and a shower of broken sharks' teeth, which you can catch in your hand as they float down.

at a glance

Local sites	10+
Level	Easy to advanced
Visibility	100ft outside reef; 40ft inside reef
Must-dives	Muri Muri, Tapu, Tupitipiti
Snorkelling	Superb on house reef, very good from dive boat
Wetsuits	3mm
Coral	Excellent
Marine life	Grey reef shark, lemon shark, black-tip reef shark, manta ray, eagle ray, schools of barracuda, humpback whale, tuna, Napoleon wrasse, dolphin
Other	Hyperbaric chamber on Tahiti (1 hr), night dives

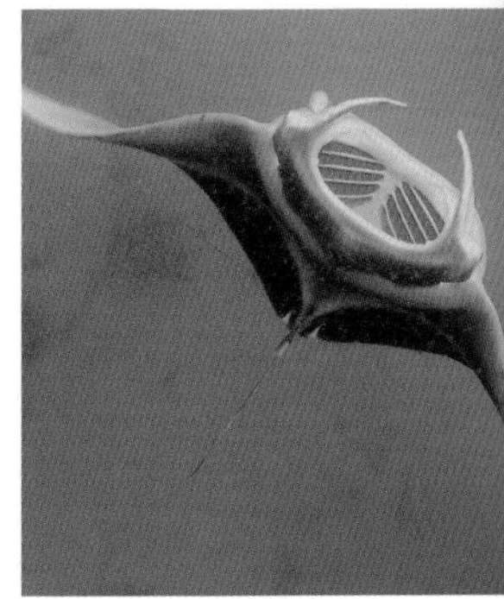

ABOVE
A feeding manta ray, seen on an afternoon snorkel.

RIGHT
Snorkelling from the hotel dock, you can swim with families of beautiful spotted eagle ray.

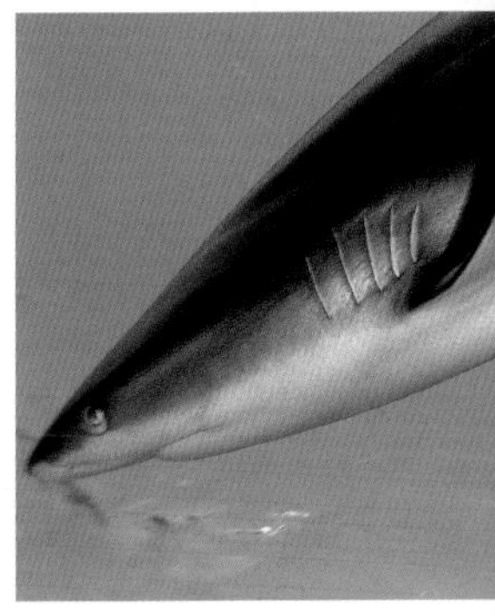

ABOVE
An inquisitive grey reef shark.

ABOVE
A wary porcupinefish, which can balloon to several times its normal size when frightened.

RIGHT
A feeding frenzy of grey reef shark at Muri Muri; diving really doesn't get better than this.

BELOW
A nighttime snorkel at the hotel dock guarantees you a close encounter with a manta ray.

ABOVE

They may not be the most colourful in the world, but Bora Bora's hard corals are in excellent condition.

BELOW

There are at least fifteen species of moray in French Polynesia. The giant moray can grow over 9ft long.

If manta are your main reason for coming to these islands, you can do no better than to don snorkel and mask at the hotel dock after sunset. Two powerful underwater lights attract the plankton, and without fail, in comes at least one manta ray. Whether you watch from the safety of the dock or dip into the water to be brushed by their wingtips, it is a truly magical experience. You can also venture to Anau, a dive site within the lagoon where manta are again drawn in by plankton; visibility varies, but it is a thrill simply to be underwater with these magnificent creatures.

A shallow clownfish dive within the reef offers orange and blood-red anemones hosting oversize, camera-shy clownfish. If visibility is good, you can swim away from the wall and over the sandy bottom, and if you're lucky, you'll be rewarded with the sight of a fifty-strong fleet of spotted eagle ray. If you're a snorkeller, then the drop-off by the hotel's overwater bungalows is amazing: you're almost guaranteed to see families of rays, brilliantly adaptive octopuses, turtles and a plethora of tropical fish.

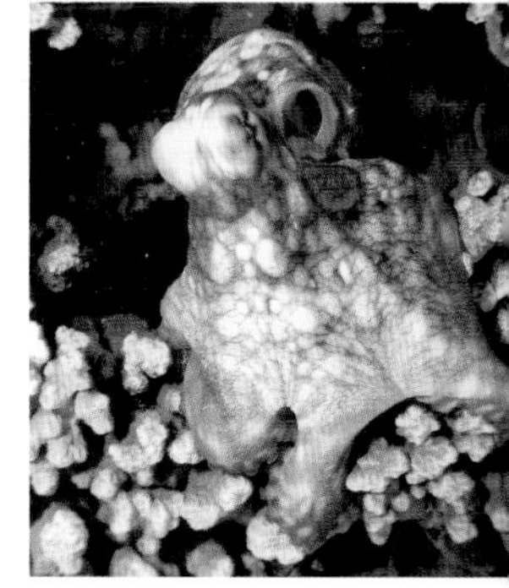

ABOVE

An octopus can change both its colour and skin texture to blend in with the corals.

BELOW

Anemones are a safe haven for many clownfish varieties, which are protected from their sting by a mucus coating.

RIGHT

There are few things more thrilling than swimming with sharks – diving at Muri Muri is like being in a movie.

BELOW

Anemones come in incredible colours. When not feeding, they fold in on themselves to become iridescent spheres.

The main island of Tikehau isn't much to look at – it's a remote coral atoll whose flat surface never rises more than a few inches above sea level. But don't be fooled by appearances: it's worth coming here for the diving alone. What's more, just a fifteen-minute boat ride away is the small private motu that is home to the luxurious Pearl Beach Resort.

tikehau

HOTEL pearl beach tikehau

Established in 1990, this oasis of a resort was substantially remodelled and expanded in 2001. Built in the traditional Polynesian style, with palm-thatched roofs and woven bamboo walls, it now boasts thirty-eight rooms. Virtually all have air-conditioning, but the island's constant wind and efficient ceiling fans mean you probably won't need it. Leave doors and windows open and you will be lulled to sleep by the sound of lapping water, as that is all there is to hear.

You can choose to stay on the beach or over the water. The beach bungalows are set amid waving palms on a thin strip of pinkish sand, which is not exactly powdery but does offer good shallow swimming and snorkelling; these rooms are all the same size and feature raised decks and internal–external bathrooms. The overwater rooms come as standard bungalows, most of which enjoy views over the lagoon, and premium bungalows, which have the added plus of direct access to the lagoon.

For the best and biggest rooms, make a beeline for the newest overwater suites. These are reached via a 300ft timber walkway stretching over the transparent lagoon, and are even more tranquil; for the ultimate in seclusion, opt for room 45 at the very end of the

at a glance

Airport	Tikehau via Papeete
Airlines	Air New Zealand, Air Tahiti Nui, Qantas, Air France
Transfer time	15 mins by boat
Rooms	38 (most air-conditioned)
Staff ratio	3+
Activities	Bird island trip, village trip, desert island picnics, kayaking, swimming pool, volleyball, *pétanque*
Services	Telephone, television, CD player, room service
Children	12+
Power type	2-pin round
Currency	French Pacific franc, US dollar
GMT	-10
Telephone	+689 962300
Website	www.pearlresorts.com/tikehau
Booking	www.diveinstyle.com

resort. These overwater suites host a generous sitting area, wooden floors and a pair of French doors that give onto your own private deck. This is spacious enough to accommodate two comfy wooden loungers along with a covered eating area, and is oriented to provide total privacy. A lower-level swimming platform has a shower and steps leading into the water – snorkelling couldn't be easier. Wake up early and you might catch some small (harmless) black-tip reef sharks or eagle rays in the sands and coral heads beneath you.

People staying in the beach bungalows are often puzzled as to why, after an excellent dinner, fellow guests can be seen shamelessly ferrying large portions of French bread back to their rooms. The mystery is solved by a look inside the overwater rooms: the design incorporates a glass floor panel that not only gives a view of the lagoon below, but also lets you drop bread through a small adjacent hatchway. This is a novel way of creating a feeding frenzy, but in fact you're better off throwing bread from the deck – you'll create just as much mayhem and get a much better view of the fish.

It's not just the fish that are well fed here; the guests are too. One of the great things about this part of the world is the French influence, especially when it comes to food. Breakfast includes fresh croissants, baguettes and *pains au chocolat*, while other meals, served at the Porteho restaurant, are all based around a simple but delicious French-inspired menu that usually focuses on fresh local fish. The choice makes perfect sense in light of the cost of importing goods here; most things, including meat, have to travel from as far away as Australia or New Zealand. But so pampered are you at Pearl Beach that it's easy to forget the logistics behind the luxury.

All over the resort, the atmosphere is low-key and relaxed, with no apparent dress code. If you want to use the resort as a chill zone, you can lie on the sand or in the small freshwater infinity pool by the beach, and gaze out over the gin-clear waters of the sea; if you'd rather venture elsewhere, there is a limited range of activities available, from line fishing to lunch on a deserted motu. Whatever your priorities, Pearl Beach offers a true escape.

140
SUZUKI
140

Squeezed next door to the front desk of Pearl Beach Tikehau, the dive center is small but perfectly placed. Run by English-speaking French instructors, it's a laid-back affair, and you're given the shortest indemnity form you're ever likely to sign. The briefing is simple: the main point is that by law the maximum diving depth is 100ft unless you are suitably qualified.

DIVE CENTER

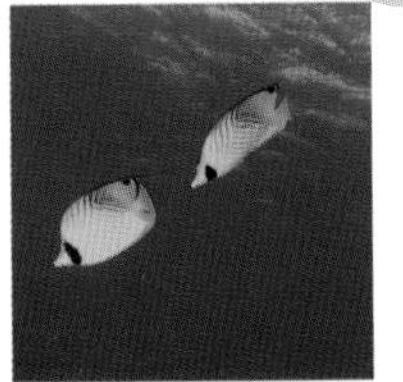

Dives are generally in the morning to take advantage of the sunlight, and a two-tank trip departs daily. You can choose from a good selection of Sherwood equipment; it is up to you to rig and then rinse it at the end of the day. The staff will stow and prepare it for your next excursion, but that is about the limit of it.

The boat is no-frills but adequate, and can take up to twelve divers. Space is somewhat limited and there is no real allowance for underwater cameras, although there is a small dry compartment. The dive sites are only a twenty-five-minute ride across the lagoon, but be prepared to get wet if the sea gets choppy; you would be best advised to don your wetsuit before boarding.

Entry is by backward roll, but if you wish, the captain will help you put on and remove your gear in the water. Groups are of no more than five, a fact that enhances your sense of pathfinding, and dives are normally limited to about fifty minutes. Tea, water and biscuits are served during the surface intervals.

In short, this is a fairly basic dive operation that gets the job done. The most important thing is to remember where you are: you won't see another dive boat, so the sites are truly yours.

at a glance

Boats	24ft (wet, covered)
Group size	5
Instructors	2
Languages	English, French
Courses	Qualification dives and advanced courses; no beginners' courses
Children	12+
Other	Drinks, gear prep
Website	www.bluenui.com

ABOVE

Acres of stunning virgin coral greet you every time you dive Tikehau's translucent waters.

The dive operation may be simple, but this hardly matters once you are underwater. The atoll of Tikehau was once described by Jacques Cousteau as richer in fish life than any other lagoon in the world. Although decades have gone by since then, it is still clearly exceptional.

DIVING

Like Rangiroa, its larger and more crowded neighbour, Tikehau has only one pass into the ocean, Tuheiva, and five out of the six dive sites are clustered around it. Luckily Pearl Beach is the only hotel in the area, so there is no competition for the moorings.

Without a doubt, Shark Hole takes the prize, and like all the sites, it has fantastic 100ft-plus visibility. As you start your descent, you're guaranteed to see dozens of grey reef sharks circling beneath you; they will generally approach within 6ft, and nearer if you're not looking. You're also bound to spot a friendly Napoleon wrasse gliding back and forth; it will also come quite close, though never quite close enough to show off its brilliant colouring. Turn to the wall itself and you'll see that it's literally alive, undulating with thousands upon thousands of squirrelfish.

Once you've made your way past these and the occasional hawksbill turtle, you end up in a spectacular coral garden. French Polynesia has no soft corals but it has good claim to be the world's hard coral capital, especially here on Tikehau with its seemingly endless fields stretching out before you. These shallow waters offer a truly fabulous sight: the sea is rarely deeper than 30ft, and it is magical being underwater in such a pristine environment.

OPPOSITE TOP

Tikehau's perfect corals provide shelter for predators and prey alike.

FAR RIGHT

A diver soars over the abyss-like drop-off with the brilliant colours of a basket star in the foreground.

OPPOSITE MIDDLE

Butterflyfish are almost always seen in pairs. Most keep the same mate for life.

OPPOSITE RIGHT

Moray eels are cleaned by trusting fish and shrimp. Their open mouths may look aggressive, but don't be put off: this is how they breathe.

at a glance

Local sites	6
Level	Easy
Visibility	100ft+
Must-dives	Shark Hole
Snorkelling	Very good from dive boat
Wetsuits	3mm
Coral	Pristine
Marine life	Grey reef shark, black-tip reef shark, hammerhead shark, white-tip reef shark, Napolean wrasse, dolphin, schools of jackfish, schools of African pompanos, eagle ray
Other	Hyperbaric chamber on Tahiti (1 hr)

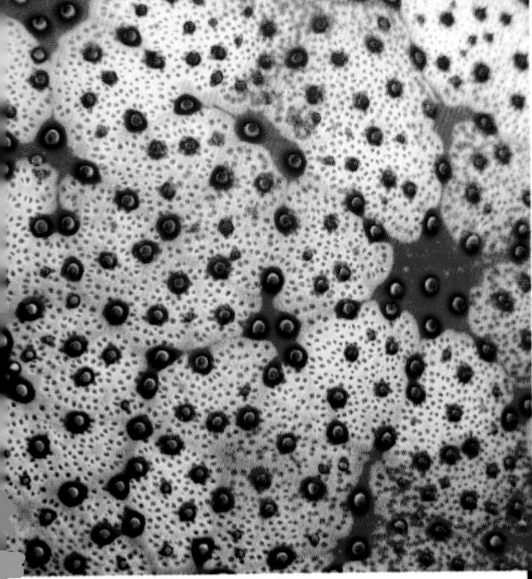

RIGHT
The walls at Tikehau can be literally alive with fish.

BELOW RIGHT
Close encounters with grey and black-tip reef shark are guaranteed at Shark Hole.

ABOVE
A close-up of the beautifully-patterned basket star.

LEFT
Inquisitive Napoleon wrasse appear on nearly every dive.

RIGHT
The reef's craggy surface provides endless hidden vantage points for predators such as lionfish, scorpionfish and stonefish.

Almost as good is a site without a name right on the edge of Tuheiva Pass. Again, you'll discover vast fields of perfect hard coral – surely this is what all the world's reefs looked like before pollution and global warming. This is an easy dive, as always to a maximum of 100ft, and you'll find countless lionfish hiding in the overhangs, some truly enormous stonefish wedged into impossible nooks, the ever-present Napoleon wrasse, the occasional hammerhead and a plethora of multicoloured fish. Green morays are in abundance – it's not uncommon to see four or five at a time – but watch out if you're looking for a handhold on dead coral as these creatures possess the unfortunate combination of poor eyesight and sharp teeth.

In good weather you can explore the open sea just behind the hotel (although this is difficult to get to), while on a rising tide you can go on a fast drift dive through Tuheiva pass; the latter is a must, as it brings with it all manner of life including manta ray and hammerheads. This is remote, unspoilt diving where anything can turn up, and drifting over acres of virgin coral in translucent waters, knowing there is no one else for miles, adds an edge to every dive.

costa rica

Independent since 1821, the Republic of Costa Rica is Central America's jewel of stability, the most settled of the often somewhat troubled nations in the region. Located between Nicaragua and Panama, Costa Rica's two coastlines border the waters of the Caribbean and Pacific respectively, while in between lie some truly beautiful rainforests as well as a string of volcanoes. A number of these are still active; Arenal volcano in particular, a two-hour drive from the Papagayo Peninsula, provides an almost nightly firework display.

If you have already explored the best of Central America's Caribbean shore to the east, the west coast will give you a totally different experience, at least from a dive perspective. The narrow strip that connects the two Americas also separates two totally different marine habitats. The Pacific's nutrient-rich waters are wilder and cooler than those of the Caribbean, but they attract a blizzard of sea life; washing up from the south, they also bathe the Galapagos. You almost wonder whether the country's Spanish settlers had early access to scuba gear when they named it the 'Rich Coast'.

Nowhere represents this better than the Papagayo Peninsula, which lets you access it all in style. A sliver of land in the northwest corner of one of Costa Rica's least developed areas, it is home to the country's first truly five-star resort, the Four Seasons Peninsula Papagayo.

The 2,400-acre Papagayo Peninsula is part of a giant, government-backed development project on Costa Rica's Pacific coast. One day it will be peppered with resorts, but for the moment the Four Seasons has this shore all to itself, occupying its finest location. Years ago this was virgin forest; nowadays howler monkeys steal balls from the Arnold Palmer golf course and iguanas dice with the hotel's immaculate SUVs.

papagayo peninsula

RESORT

four seasons peninsula papagayo

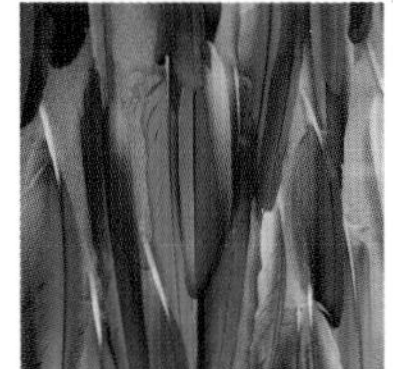

From the airport of Liberia, a thirty-minute drive takes you to what looks to be the entrance to the hotel's grounds, announced by a stand of perfect palms. In fact this is the gateway to the peninsula. For five miles a brick road winds between forest and fairway until you reach the hub of the resort, flanked by a beach on either side. Of the two, the rather enthusiastically named Playa Blanca is not *blanca* at all, but rather 'greya'; Playa Virador is an altogether better bet. Both, however, offer calm, protected swimming.

Apparently designed to look like the lip of a terracotta pot, with rooms inspired by the shape of an armadillo, some may quibble with the resort's architectural aesthetic. Nonetheless, it is certainly different and successfully blends in with its surroundings.

The 123 rooms are arranged in three large wings, while the more upscale lodgings and suites are scattered in clusters on the hillside. The standard rooms are generous in size and beautifully furnished, featuring a typically faultless Four Seasons bed decked with fabulous linens, a spacious bathroom and a sort of inside–outside sitting room protected by an almost invisible mosquito screen. It is worth paying extra to stay on one of the upper floors, as the views are spectacular; lower down you have only a glimpse of water.

at a glance

Airport	Liberia
Airlines	American Airlines, Continental Airlines, Delta Airlines, United Airlines
Transfer time	45 mins by car from Liberia
Rooms	163 rooms and suites (all air-conditioned)
Staff ratio	4
Activities	Golf, nature tours, fishing, sailing, kayaking, rainforest canopy tours, white-water rafting, surfing, children's programmes, tennis, gym, spa, swimming pools
Services	Television, internet, room service
Children	All ages
Power type	2-pin flat
Currency	Costa Rican colon, US dollar
GMT	-6
Telephone	+506 6960000
Website	www.fourseasons.com
Booking	www.diveinstyle.com

The three restaurants are overseen by the incredibly attentive staff; nothing is too much trouble. Breakfast is served in the brasserie, lunch either there or by the pool at Congos, and dinner at either of these, with the added option of elegant Italian restaurant Mare. The MAP (Modified American Plan) rate offers a good deal, though be sure to have the rules fully explained. Argentinian night at Congos is a particular treat, with a constant stream of fabulous barbecued meat and fish, guaranteed to satisfy anyone's appetite.

There is plenty to do, with special programmes for kids. For instance, expeditions to different rainforests give you a chance to see howler monkeys and scarlet macaws (though skip the 'skywalk' day excursion), while the resort offers a nonstop flow of activities, from Pilates to surfing and white-water rafting. Staying here, you benefit from all the service, style and comfort that has come to be synonymous with the Four Seasons name, along with distinctive architecture set against a stunning natural backdrop. Accommodation of this quality, in previously the poorest and most untouched part of Costa Rica, is an achievement in itself.

mares

Diving at the Four Seasons Peninsula Papagayo is simplicity itself. Run by an American family, Diving Safaris is a fifteen-minute boat ride across the bay, not that you will ever have to visit. At 9 a.m. you leave for a two-tank dive from Playa Blanca, the hotel's own beach, and the team is always on time.

DIVE CENTER

A small boat takes you from the beach's edge to one of Diving Safaris' fleet of five boats. Though simple, the vessels are perfectly comfortable and fine for their task, especially considering that most of the dive sites are close by. The only exceptions are the Bat and Catalina Islands, both of which are really day trips, but not to worry – Diving Safaris are equipped with the right boats to deal with longer journeys.

Only basic refreshments are offered on the boat, usually water, fruit and biscuits. But unless you go on a day trip, you normally return to the Four Seasons by 1 p.m., which leaves you plenty of time to have lunch at the resort.

The dive guides more than make up for any shortcomings in the food department, always doing their utmost to show you the best of the local exotics. As for your gear, you don't have to worry about it; they rig it, swap bottles after the first dive, then take it all away; the following day you find it on the boat, rinsed and ready to go.

Diving Safaris run Bubblemaker courses for kids in the hotel pool, and every Friday they also host an introduction to scuba for adults. It's a perfect opportunity to get hooked.

at a glance

Boats	25ft+ (wet/dry, covered)
Group size	6
Instructors	5
Languages	English, Spanish
Courses	All PADI
Children	12+
Other	Nitrox and rebreathers (24 hrs notice), some food and drink, gear prep and wash down, private charters
Website	www.costaricadiving.net

ABOVE
The reefs are teeming with porcupinefish. Unfortunately their favourite snack is the beautiful and incredibly appealing seahorse.

If you're bent on seeing coral, then the diving off Papagayo is not for you; the same goes for the Galapagos and much of this eastern part of the Pacific. If, on the other hand, you're after some amazing marine life, you won't be disappointed – Papagayo is a bit like a junior Galapagos. This is the finest diving on Central America's Pacific coast, with the exception of the Cocos Islands, a few hundred miles offshore and only reachable by live-aboard.

DIVING

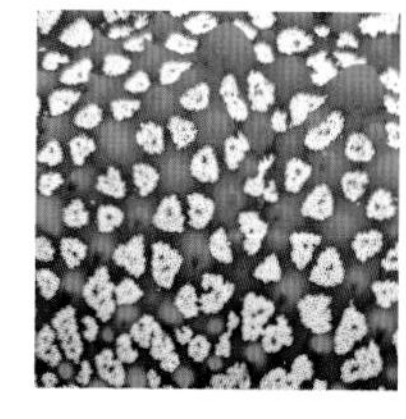

The sites near Papagayo aren't so different from the Cocos Islands in terms of topography, with a gently sloping sea bed covered in endless boulders, large and small, which in turn are dressed in algae, some small soft corals and the occasional hard coral. They also host some fantastic sea life. A few minutes from the Four Seasons, Virador presents a smorgasbord of unusual species, while at Argentina you can take on the challenge of spotting one of its large orange frogfish.

Before diving Papagayo, two small but perfectly formed stars of the marine world had proved elusive: the incredibly appealing seahorse and the somewhat 'bling' harlequin clown shrimp. On the first dive at Virador, not only did they show up, but they brought company: arrestingly beautiful sea urchins, eagle ray, devil ray, jewel moray, snowflake moray, loggerhead turtle, scorpionfish, milkfish and vast schools of grunts, all set to a haunting soundtrack of whale song.

Further afield, you are virtually guaranteed a pulse-racing close encounter with large – and I do mean large – bull shark at the famous Bat Islands. Head south to the more dramatic diving of the Catalinas and you will find giant schools of cownose ray, literally in their thousands. Another Catalina speciality is the stunning but

at a glance

Local sites	22
Level	Easy to advanced
Visibility	20–40ft (December–March), 20–70ft (April–November)
Must-dives	Virador, Bat Islands, Catalinas Islands
Snorkelling	Average from Playa Blanca, good from dive boat
Wetsuits	3mm in summer, 5mm in winter
Coral	Poor
Marine life	Harlequin clown shrimp, seahorse, jewel and zebra moray, bull and whale shark, eagle, devil and manta ray, schools of cownose ray, ridley, green and leatherback turtle, large schools of grunt, spade and jackfish, frogfish, pilot, humpback and killer whale
Other	Day trips, night dives, hyperbaric chamber (1.5 hrs), marine park at Bat Islands

OPPOSITE TOP, LEFT TO RIGHT
Snowflake moray, for once out of their lairs and on the hunt; seahorses are normally hard to find but have made their homes on a number of local reefs; the stunning but shy zebra moray, one of the more snake-like of the species, and common in the Catalinas.

OPPOSITE MAIN PICTURE
The extraordinary harlequin shrimp eat only starfish, a sort of living larder. They gorge on them for weeks, clinging on and feasting from the tube feet in.

LEFT
The jewel moray, one of the more beautiful members of the family found in Costa Rica's waters.

BELOW LEFT
A stunning starfish, dull until seen in artificial light – a good reason to always dive with a flashlight.

OPPOSITE TOP, LEFT TO RIGHT
There is so much marine life that it is possible to lose your buddy in a flurry of fish; juvenile white-tip reef shark regularly hide out in caves; there is no shortage of schooling fish, perhaps because of the lack of commercial fishing.

OPPOSITE, MAIN PICTURE
White-tip reef shark can grow quite large, as proven by this pregnant female.

reclusive zebra moray, almost commonplace here. And there's always the possibility of coming across any number of larger species, including Pacific manta ray, whale shark, killer whale, pilot whale and humpback whale.

At any of the sites, you stand a genuine chance of losing your diving buddy in a flurry of fish. This is no exaggeration – the schools of grunt, spade and jackfish are truly enormous. The water may not be perfectly clear and the underwater landscape could be more striking, but the marine life here is simply exceptional; it deserves a place on the 'must-dive' list of any diver who has not yet ventured to the eastern Pacific.

The water temperature and visibility here is varied. The abundance of marine life is fed by the currents that sweep up from the cold upwellings to the south, so it's not unusual to have quite extreme variations. For the best overall conditions, it's best to dive during the summer wet season, when visibility is up to 70ft; there is usually a shower in the afternoon, and it tends to be somewhat cloudy. But if you want to try to see killer whales, the huge Pacific manta ray or whale shark, then you will probably want to don a 5mm wetsuit and come when the water is cooler, although the visibility drops as the cold water brings in the plankton.

If you can't bear the thought of a live-aboard, the diving nirvanas of the Cocos and Galapagos Islands are out of reach. Luckily, Papagayo comes close to the experience, while still allowing you to sleep in one of the best hotel beds in the world.

mexico

Mexico has two totally different coastlines, one on the Pacific, the other on the Caribbean. While the Pacific side is battered by the ocean and best known for resort towns such as Acapulco and Puerta Vallarta, the Caribbean coast offers calm waters and pure white-sand beaches, and is home to the Riviera Maya on the Yucatán Peninsula.

Cancún, the peninsula’s main city, is the jumping-off

The brainchild of architect Jean Louis Moreno, Hotel Maroma is nestled within a five-hundred-acre coconut plantation blessed with a secluded bay and the finest white-sugar sand beach on the Riviera Maya. Although the property has changed hands and is now part of the Orient Express group, the hotel remains true to Moreno's vision. What's more, tight controls mean Maroma still enjoys the best and least-developed strip of real estate on Mexico's Caribbean coast.

Wherever you sleep, you're never more than a few steps away from the palapa-lined beach. And what a beach: two miles of perfect white powder, gently descending to the calm, protected waters of the bay. An inviting array of luxury beach furniture, including comfy chairs, loungers and large daybeds strewn with oversized cushions, ensures you'll want to stay put. And why shouldn't you? Say the word and you'll be brought everything from breakfast and lunch to a romantic torch-lit supper. You could spend your whole stay on the beach and not have to lift a finger.

If you can tear yourself away from the sand, it's worth venturing to Puerto Aventuras, a small town thirty minutes south of Maroma and probably the only place in the world where you'll have the chance to swim with dolphins, sting rays and manatees at the same time. You're also free to explore the magical Mayan ruins of Tulum or Chichen Itza, ride a horse through the jungle, go deep-sea fishing or even sky-dive.

Where you eat is up to you, but there are few places better than the main terrace. Just on the beach's edge, this is where you'll find the open-air dining area shaded by soaring palms and with views onto the multi-hued ocean. The dress code is basically casual, but while in the day informality rules, at night a little more elegance is required. The food at lunch and dinner is a fusion of Mexican and European, but breakfast is a particular treat – fresh juices and homemade jams from the exotic local fruit, as well as creamy pancakes with cinnamon syrup.

No description of Maroma would be complete without a mention of the temazcal, an ancient Aztec ritual of spiritual and physical cleansing carried out here every evening. It is not for the faint-hearted: you descend into a dark, semi-buried steam room while you listen to the sound of traditional incantations. Though it may not be for everyone, it's certainly an experience.

One of the best things about Maroma is that even when it's fully booked, you'll wonder where all the guests went. The beachside dining room is rarely more than half full, there's always space under a palapa and never a crowd at the bar – or anywhere for that matter. Regardless of when you come, the place feels wonderfully empty.

TURTLE NEST
NIDO DE TORTUGA

This tiny diving outfit is run by what must be the most knowledgeable, friendly and experienced team on the entire Caribbean coastline. Ramón has been diving the sites here for years – in fact, he helped discover them – and he and his team know every inch of these reefs intimately. Diving is their life, and like underwater bushmen, they have an eye for everything that moves.

DIVE CENTER

The diving here is highly personalized. Most dives are for only two to four guests, so you generally turn up at an appointed time of your own choosing. Departures tend to be around 9 to 9.15 a.m., when you take a short wade out to the boat, a local 22ft vessel decorated with handpainted designs by none other than Ramón's wife. While it doesn't offer much cover, this isn't a problem as all the dive sites are under ten minutes away; alternative arrangements can be made if you want to take a day trip further afield.

The center offers a selection of wetsuits and BCDs, as well as computers for hire, though it's probably best to bring your own mask. Common sense dictates that you take any computers and underwater cameras back to your room, but otherwise the center takes care of your equipment throughout your stay. Your gear awaits you when you board, rigged and ready for diving, and is rinsed and dried for your next dive once you're done for the day.

Most dives are led by the charming and watchful Ramón, who is always concerned for the safety of his guests: regardless of depth, every dive ends with a five-minute safety stop – as well as a traditional warm handshake. It's hard to think of a better place to learn to dive.

at a glance

Boats	22ft (wet, partially covered)
Group size	4
Instructors	4
Languages	English, Spanish, French
Courses	PADI
Children	16+
Other	Computer hire, drinks, nitrox and rebreathers (by prior arrangement), gear prep and wash down, private charters

ABOVE
The ungainly arrow crab seeks safety in the arms of an anemone.

The variety of the diving here is outstanding, and there are no fewer than fifteen sites within ten minutes of the dive center. There's something for everyone: beginners can explore the thriving shallow reef ledges and their tiny drop-offs, while experienced thrill-seekers can ride the famous Maroma current and dive the *cenotes* or inland sinkholes.

DIVING

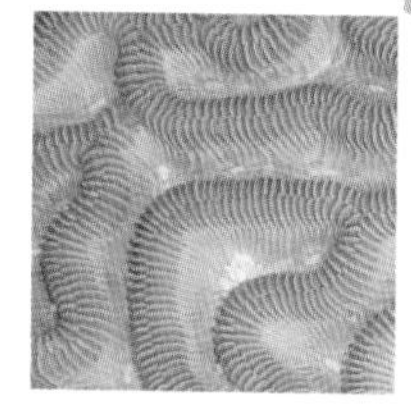

There are no real wall dives, only easy shallow dives offering mini-walls of about 10ft between plateaus, located at just 40–50ft. These are home to dense, thriving ecosystems; fan and large brain corals are especially common. Schools of grunts, rubias and the occasional rare toadfish gravitate here, and don't seem to mind the presence of divers so long as you keep your breathing slow. Spotted and green morays abound, although the latter are easier to see on night dives.

Another good dive for beginners is at New Reef. The site is a band of shallow coral some 40ft wide, with plenty of canyons and overhangs that are ideal for cruising at your own pace. Sea life abounds: you'll see yellow rays, stingrays, lobsters, parrotfish, squirrelfish, grouper and grey angelfish, among other common reef species.

If you want bigger fish, then you'll need a bit more experience. Turtle Plain is a plateau at about 100ft, which is constantly swept by the powerful Maroma current. Relatively barren and dotted with hundreds of giant sponges bent double by the relentless current, this is where large green and hawksbill turtles come to feed; while you struggle to hang on to a rock or sponge, they seem to glide effortlessly against the flow of water.

at a glance

Local sites	12
Level	Easy to advanced
Visibility	70ft+
Must-dives	Cenotes, Maroma drift dive
Snorkelling	Good on house reef, excellent on dolphin and manatee expedition
Wetsuits	3mm
Coral	Very good
Marine life	Large green and hawksbill turtle, terminal phase parrotfish, bull, nurse and whale shark, dolphin, manatee, toadfish
Other	Day trips during whale-shark season, night dives, hyperbaric chamber at Playa del Carmen (15 mins)

ABOVE
The coral reefs of the Yucatán Peninsula host over five hundred species of fish, including rubia.

FAR RIGHT
The Grand Cenote, a cavern dive accessible even to novice divers. It's difficult to believe this is actually underwater.

MIDDLE
Jaws agape, a grouper hovers at a cleaning station.

RIGHT
Most species of grouper flush or colour up when being cleaned.

LEFT
The shallow, protected waters of New Reef give you the opportunity for long, easy dives.

BELOW LEFT
While a turtle floats effortlessly, grazing in the Maroma's strong currents, a diver struggles to maintain station.

Those looking for an adrenaline rush can do no better than the Maroma drift dive. You're dropped off in deep water and descend to nearly 130ft, where you pick up the current and fly past turtles along the top of a 6,000ft wall. In the gloom you can make out what at first seem to be lost Napoleon wrasse. In fact, these are giant terminal-phase parrotfish, whose brilliant colours grow dazzling as you near them; they pass all too quickly as you are swept along by the current.

Further afield, manatee and dolphin await you at Puerto Aventuras, while in July and August you can swim or snorkel with whale sharks at Holbox Island. The hotel also offers a day trip to two remarkable cenotes: Grande Cenote, near the Mayan ruin of Tulum, followed by Angelitas, a private cenote accessible only to Maroma.

Although you can snorkel at Grande Cenote, it needs to be dived for full effect. More cavern diving than cave diving, it offers seemingly endless visibility: as you drop into the water, you're struck first by its coolness relative to the sea, and then by its pure transparency. Following your guide, you weave your way through stalactites and stalagmites; in between caverns, you catch magical glimpses of sunlight through the deep turquoise water.

After a surface interval at Tulum, you arrive at the extraordinary site of Angelitas, a 200ft-wide sinkhole. Diving here is magical: there is no sea life to marvel at, only fallen trees, but strangely enough this only adds to the atmosphere. Once you descend through some 15ft of brackish water, you reach total clarity, and at 90ft you're greeted with a scene straight out of *Lord of the Rings*. It comes close to being in a fairytale. Magical.

LEFT
There is no shortage of fish life, fed by the nutrient-rich currents.

BELOW
The majestic eagle ray, a regular sight on the drop-off.

RIGHT
Octopus can take on an amazing range of colours and textures in their quest for anonymity.

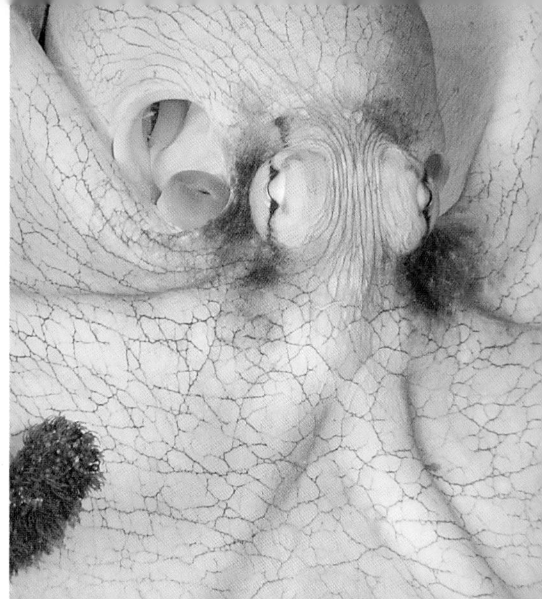

usa

The Florida Keys are a lot like the Caribbean – except you can get here by car. It's worth the trip just for the drive. Made up of over two hundred islands, thirty-four of which are inhabited, the Keys are linked by the scenic Overseas Highway (also known as US 1), 112 miles of single-lane road and forty-three bridges spanning the endless turquoise waters. When you reach the end, you are closer to Havana than Miami.

If Henry Flagler had had his way, you could keep on driving. Until 1912 there was no connecting road to the Keys. But Flagler, a tycoon and railroad developer, noticed that Key West was then the only deep-water port on the USA's southeastern coast. Hoping to take advantage of its proximity to the Panama Canal, he privately funded a causeway and railway connecting the islands and the mainland. He even got as far as building a seven-mile section towards Cuba before the Labour Day Hurricane of 1935, the strongest ever to hit the east coast, washed away most of his work.

The first of the Keys is Key Largo, where the roadside is littered with dive shops and quirky stores. Over a hundred miles down is colourful Key West, Hemingway's most famous haunt and the furthest south of all American cities, its deadpan spirit encapsulated by a famous local tombstone marked 'I told you I was sick'. But if you're looking for a luxury escape, the place to go lies in-between: Little Palm Island, just off Little Torch Key.

It's hardly surprising that the makers of *PT 109*, the classic movie about President Kennedy's wartime experiences, chose Little Palm Island to fool cinemagoers into thinking it was shot in the South Pacific. This is five acres of film-set perfection. Over a hundred miles from Miami, the island is a short boat ride from the Keys' arterial road, but it seems a lifetime away.

little palm island

HOTEL little palm island

From a discreet reception lodge on Little Torch Key, a private 1930s-style motorboat transports you ten thousand miles in just ten minutes – or at least it seems that way. Once you are immersed in the stylish and luxurious world that is Little Palm Island, it is seriously difficult to believe you are still in Florida, let alone the US.

The first thing that strikes you is the island's luxuriant vegetation. Then you notice the constant sound of birdsong. Little Palm is home to the most incredible diversity of migrating birds you can imagine, including herons, egrets, hawks, parakeets, doves, pelicans and cormorants – it's like stepping into an outdoor aviary. Nowhere else in the Keys will you find this phenomenon, and even the Audubon Society for bird protection acknowledges that this is very special.

At the heart of the resort is an intimate palm-fringed pool, which is overlooked by the Palapa Bar, the restaurant, a cosy library and a boutique. All are housed in irregular single-storey, rough timber-clad structures that give the place the feel of a private house with outbuildings. It's easy to forget you're at a hotel.

A perfect white-sand path runs around the perimeter of the complex, and off this lie twenty-eight raised, thatched-roof bungalow suites,

at a glance

Airport	Miami or Key West
Airlines	American Airlines, Continental Airlines, Delta Airlines, US Air
Transfer time	40 mins from Key West or 2.5 hrs from Miami by car, then 10 mins by boat
Rooms	28 rooms, 2 suites (all air-conditioned)
Staff ratio	4
Activities	Watersports, excursions to Key West, gym, spa, swimming pool
Services	Limited room service
Children	16+
Power type	2-pin flat
Currency	US dollar
GMT	-5
Telephone	+305 8722524
Website	www.littlepalmisland.com
Booking	www.diveinstyle.com

all with ocean views, and all private. The sense of South Seas remoteness is taken further with no in-room phones or televisions, a brave move in North America. The rooms feature vaulted ceilings, a bed draped in mosquito netting, a sitting room, whirlpool bathtubs, indoor and outdoor showers and a small private veranda. What's more, they are filled with generous touches such as your own personalized letter paper, a teddy bear on the bed and an open bar. It's like staying with a friend, only better.

The dining room is perched on a small sandy point, and it's up to you whether you eat in the air-conditioned interior, the shade overlooking the beach, or on the water's edge. Dinner is also served on the sand by the light of guttering torches, so you can watch the sun sink and the pelicans dive as you sample the sensational food. Just when you think things can't get any better, a rare Key deer, an endangered species, nuzzles up to you for food. By now you will have appreciated that Little Palm is something of an eco-sanctuary.

That said, the beach looks better than it is. The Keys aren't far from the Bahamas, but they are not blessed with the same great beaches, so don't expect Turks and Caicos-style swimming. Instead you can try something a bit different: lie back on the boardwalk or at one of the secluded spots that dot the island, or take a small boat out to explore the mangroves; if you're lucky you will find manatees, which come to Little Palm for the sea grass, their favourite food. If you want to go further afield, the dive center offers eco-kayaking tours to the Great White Heron National Wildlife Refuge.

This is a superbly run resort, with a staff-to-guest ratio more in keeping with the Far East than the West. Its location is unbeatable, the wildlife amazing and the environment unusual – it couldn't be further from your mainstream American hotel. There are no cars here; the only sounds are the splash of fishing pelicans and the occasional passing boat. It's the perfect base for exploring the Keys, and there is no place better for discovering the area's best diving.

Tides
Wind
Seas
Air Temp.
Water Temp.
L-10:27 am
15 to 20 KTS
3'-7'/1'-2'
68°-80°
76°

Island Girl
Little Palm Island
Truman Arrival Dock
Snorkel-Dive Service
Registered Guests Only
Beyond this Point

Located in Little Palm Island's sheltered harbour, where Hollywood's *PT 109* used to dock, this dive center is just behind the spa and, like everything else, a short walk from any of the rooms. It may be small, but it has an excellent range of equipment that is regularly replaced. The whole operation is designed to make diving here as painless as possible.

DIVE CENTER

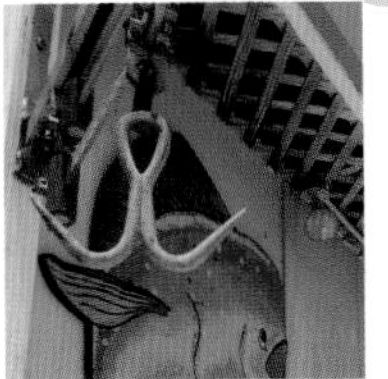

The immaculate 28ft *Island Girl* can carry up to fourteen people, but given the size of the resort its full capacity is rarely put to the test; in any case, dive groups are kept to a maximum of six. It's quite a wet boat, so it's a good idea to carry a dry bag.

Since sites such as Looe Key and the *Adolphus Busch* are very close, there is no need for catered day trips. Nonetheless, the boat always carries cold drinks and plenty of towels. If you feel chilly after a long dive (you can easily spend ninety minutes underwater at Looe Key), you even get to wear a long, lined waterproof overcoat that is guaranteed to keep you warm. This is one boat you will never get cold on, regardless of conditions – all eventualities have been covered.

The center also makes it easy for you to dive further afield. If you have time to take in the *Thunderbolt* wreck up in Marathon, you will be driven thirty minutes or so north to the small but perfectly organized Deep Blue Dive Center. This runs you out to the site some twenty minutes away, and then to a second, shallower dive. If you want to make a day of it, on your way back you can stop for lunch at one of the many restaurants overlooking the ocean. In short, this is a quality set-up and a seamless extension to the resort.

at a glance

Boats	28ft+ (wet, covered)
Group size	6
Instructors	2
Languages	English
Courses	All PADI
Children	16+
Other	Nitrox, rebreathers, drinks, gear prep and wash down, private charters, underwater scooter hire

ABOVE
The wrecks around Little Palm provide a haven for both predator and prey. The barracuda seem particularly well fed.

There are two types of diving here. The first is gentle, shallow and very easy – ideal for beginners. The second is exciting, deep wreck diving, often swept by currents, and is only for more advanced divers. Regardless of your experience, this is excellent diving with something for everyone.

DIVING

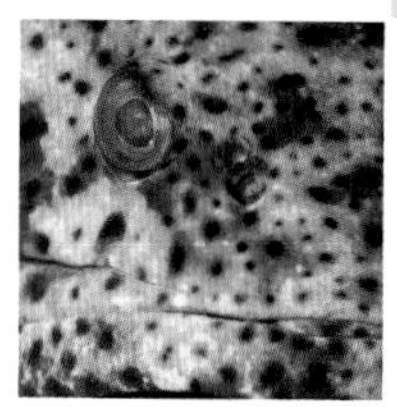

Named after the unfortunate H.M.S. *Looe* which sank on the reef in 1742, Looe Key was designated a marine reserve in 1981. Only a twenty-minute ride from the resort, it is home to some of the most spectacular spur and groove coral formations anywhere on the Keys. What's more, the turquoise waters are so clear that you'd be forgiven for thinking you were in the Bahamas. It is difficult to get much deeper than about 30ft, so this is an ideal place for both learning to dive and doing qualification dives.

While the coral is healthy, the most remarkable thing about Looe Key is that it is absolutely bursting with fish life; it's as though word has got out among fish circles that the area is protected. You'll see schools of grunt, porgy, sergeant major and goatfish, and if you're lucky, you'll be blessed with the brief but beautiful sight of a resident school of midnight parrotfish; like a scene from an underwater Hitchcock movie, these descend from nowhere in a cloud, gorging briefly on the coral before rushing on.

But that's not all. There are also grey, French and queen angelfish, barracuda, green and spotted moray. If you look under the ledges and overhangs, you may find an accommodating Goliath grouper, and looking up you might spot a reef shark or eagle ray. All this is

at a glance

Local sites	30+
Level	Easy to advanced
Visibility	80ft May–October, 30ft November–April
Must-dives	Looe Key, *Adolphus Busch*, *Thunderbolt*
Snorkelling	Very good from dive boat
Wetsuits	3mm
Coral	Good
Marine life	Bottlenose dolphin, eagle ray, black-tip, bull, nurse and reef shark, Goliath grouper, green and spotted moray, tarpon, manatee
Other	Day trips, night dives, wreck dives, marine park

OPPOSITE, CLOCKWISE FROM TOP LEFT
Schools of yellowtail are plentiful; the fish life in Looe Key marine park is some of the richest in the coastal waters of the USA; like most of their species, grey angelfish mate for life; the Florida Keys are home to an abundance of wrecks, a playground for both novices and more experienced divers.

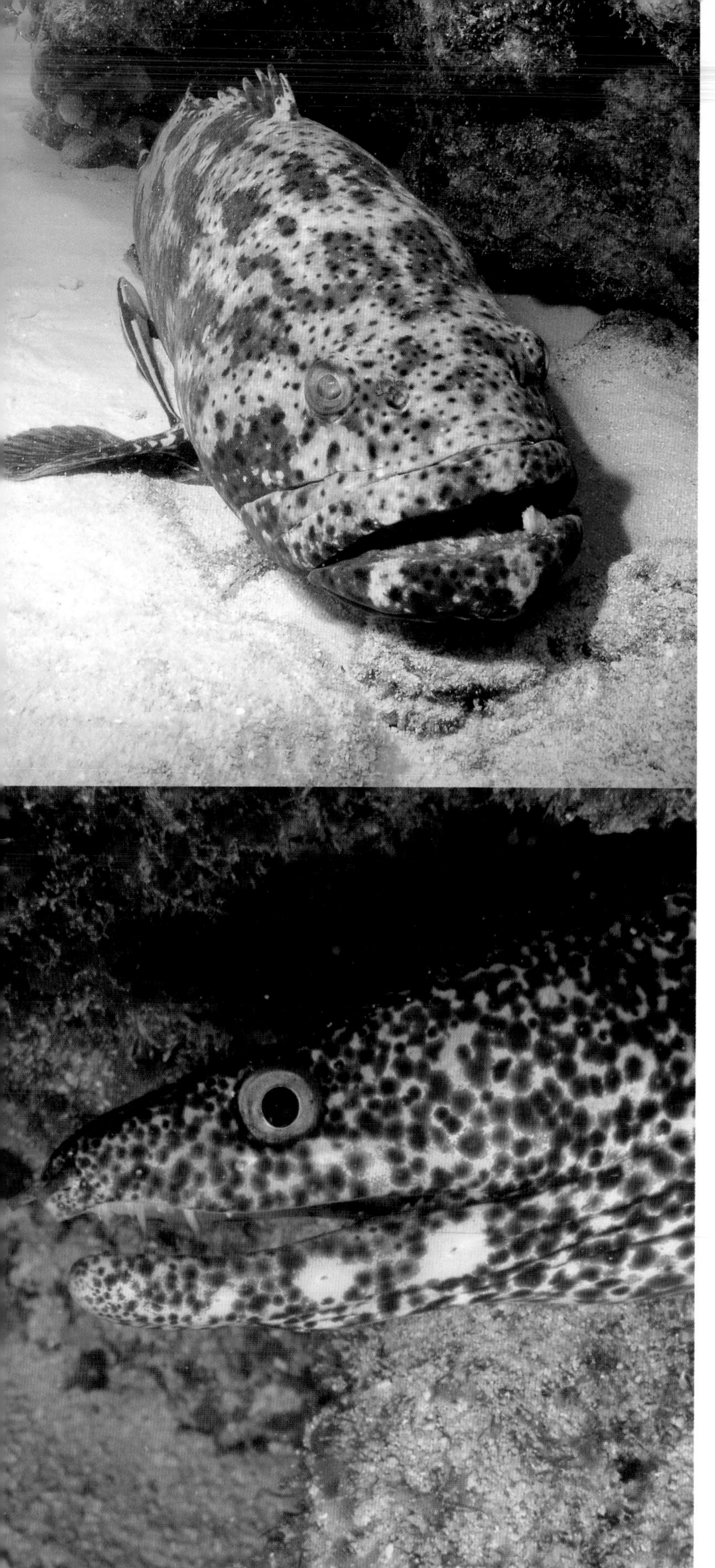

LEFT
Since fishing for them became illegal in Florida, Goliath grouper, also known as jewfish, have enjoyed a real resurgence.

BELOW LEFT
The Florida reefs are home to two kinds of eel, the green and the spotted moray.

amazing to see given you are in the USA, and one of the benefits of this dive is that it is so shallow that you can spend forever underwater just watching the sea life go by. Granted, the diving can't compare to somewhere like Indonesia or the Great Barrier Reef in terms of variety. But it is still incredibly rewarding, and beginners will see more underwater action here than at many better-known dive spots.

If you're looking for more of a challenge, then the wreck dives are for you. You can head to either the *Adolphus Busch*, a twenty-five-minute boat ride, or the *Thunderbolt* at Marathon Key, a bit further out but definitely worth the trip. These sites have varying visibility and are quite deep at around 100ft, so to get the most out of them it's best to breathe nitrox, especially given the strict local diving guidelines.

The *Adolphus Busch* lies beneath 108ft of water, while the 188ft *Thunderbolt* sits upright at 115ft. The latter was once used for studying lightning, as its name suggests; a balloon on a steel cable was floated into thunderstorms to encourage strikes. At both of these sites, you will find the reclusive giants, seriously big Goliath groupers; these are somewhat timid as they were once nearly wiped out by speargun-fishing, but they are now enjoying a comeback thanks to their new-found status as a protected species. In addition, chrome-plated 100lb tarpon glint in the water, jack hunt the droves of glassfish, and large barracuda seem to think they own the wrecks. Even if you've dived other, more spectacular sites in other parts of the world, this is wonderful diving, and it's one of the greatest and most surprising perks of staying at Little Palm.

BELOW
The monogamous grey angelfish is normally very approachable.

RIGHT
The *Thunderbolt*, one of the finest wreck dives in the Keys, finished her days as an experiment to determine the effects of lightning on ships. A tethered balloon from this very spool was floated into thunderstorms to attract lightning.

RIGHT
The aptly named four-eye butterflyfish uses its extra 'eyes' to confuse predators.

VODKA

belize

Belize has come late to tourism. A British colony until 1981 with a disputed Guatemalan border, the country only really achieved political stability in 1998. As a consequence, much of it is still untouched: there are jaguars and rainforests in the hinterland, and you'll find virgin reefs off the coast. Thankfully the government has committed to protecting these natural resources, linking up with privately funded conservation groups.

If you believe the magazines, the place to go is San Pedro. But aside from a few Disneyesque stingray and shark-feeding dives, you're bound to be disappointed: the reefs have been stripped clean by the almost annual hurricanes. You'll have better luck further south. Two hours away are the fabled Blue Hole and the Turneffe Islands; the former is interesting, but the latter offer some of the best diving in the Caribbean. However, accommodation is limited: if you're willing to accept the time penalty, you can stay at the small but chic Mata Chica in San Pedro, but five hours of daily travel is hardly diving in style.

You would do better to head even further south, where you'll come to Turtle Inn on the Placencia Peninsula. Aside from plentiful year-round sea life, in season you are guaranteed to find whale shark just an hour off the coast: this is the only place in the world where marine biologists have figured out why and exactly when these creatures turn up. For land-lovers, there's also hiking in the beautiful interior. It's an unbeatable combination.

In 2002, there was both good news and bad news for Turtle Inn. The bad news was that Hurricane Iris had almost levelled it. And the good news? Hurricane Iris had almost levelled it! This small resort was the brainchild of film director Francis Ford Coppola, and when nature presented him with a clean canvas, he used the opportunity to create a whole new resort.

placencia peninsula

HOTEL turtle inn

The approach to Turtle Inn stands out thanks to its immaculate lush green lawns. Given that the land was practically stripped bare in 2002, Coppola and his team have done a remarkable job of restoring it – you would have no idea of its recent history. The nearest town is sleepy Placencia, which lies on a peninsula a thirty-minute flight south of Belize City. Regularly serviced by efficient local airline Tropic Air, this long, narrow strip of land juts out from the coast just inches above sea level, and is sandwiched between two bodies of water: on one side it fronts the open ocean, while on the other it borders a sheltered lagoon that is home to everything from manatees to 18ft crocodiles.

Built under soaring thatched roofs, the resort features a blend of Mayan and Balinese influences. This theme runs throughout the design: carved stone reliefs, antique-style painted doors, ornate timber friezes, stone paths lined with candles... Even if you didn't know the owner's identity, you can't help but feel there's something theatrical about it all; it's a bit like an impeccable stage set.

The rooms are either directly on the beach or a thirty-second walk from it. Each is a free-standing, thatched-roofed raised hut, with a generous screened porch, a spacious sitting area, a comfortable

at a glance

Airport	Placencia via Belize City
Airlines	American, Continental, Delta or US Air, then Tropic Air/Maya Island Air to Placencia
Transfer time	3 mins by car
Rooms	25 (none air-conditioned)
Staff ratio	3+
Activities	Watersports, fishing, jaguar spotting, rainforest, swimming pool, spa
Services	Internet, room service
Other	Mobile phones allowed
Children	All ages
Power type	2-pin flat
Currency	Belizean dollar (US dollar widely accepted)
GMT	-6
Telephone	+501 8244912
Website	www.turtleinn.com
Booking	www.diveinstyle.com

bedroom and a queen-sized bed. While the bed size is surprising – there is plenty of room – this is not an oversight, as Coppola explains: 'If you are here alone you don't need a king, and if you are here with someone you love, you shouldn't want one!'

No two rooms are exactly the same. You can choose from the Honeymoon Cottage, the Chinese Matrimonial Suite, the Pavilion House, and the two-bedroom Garden or Seaview Villas (ideal for families or friends). All have a distinctly Balinese feel to them, what with their high roofs, carved doors, timber surrounds, and stone carvings and statues. Although they are not air-conditioned, they are surprisingly cool thanks to quiet but effective ceiling fans.

Although Belize's tourist board insists that Placencia has some of the country's best beaches, there is neither powder-white sand nor clear turquoise water. While the excellent staff go to great lengths to make up for this by endlessly raking the beach of seaweed, the best options for swimming are either the beautiful circular main pool or the private pool that comes with the fabulous Pavilion House villa.

Meals are usually served in the Mare Restaurant, which looks out onto the pool and ocean. The ever-obliging staff will also arrange dinner for you on the beach or in your room, while for lunch you can eat at the sand-floored Laughing Fish Bar on the beach's edge. The chef uses local ingredients, including organic produce from sister resort Blancaneaux Lodge, and he has created a menu with a distinctly Italian edge to it, reflecting Coppola's roots.

Turtle Inn is very special. True to its owner's vision, the resort has retained its own individual character, and it looks set to stay that way. You may not find perfect white-sand beaches, but you are surrounded by nature, both above and beneath the water: manatees, rainforests, waterfalls and the world's only jaguar reserve, not to mention some incredible marine life, including whale shark. There is no better place to discover all this and more.

WHALE SHARK
SAPODILLA TOM
Sightings of
Week
23rd Whale Sharks, Turtles, Dolphins
24th Whale Sharks, Turtles. Dolphins
25th Whale Sharks, Turtles, Dolphins
26th Whale Sharks, Blue Marlin!
27th Nurse Shark, Turtles, Eels, Long-spined Sea Biscuit
28th
29th Whale Sharks
1st Whale Sharks, Bull Sharks
3rd Whale Sharks, many schools of Fish!
4th Loggerhead Turtle, Spotted Eagle Ray, Eels
the Fishing Industry
Marine Life of Belize
CORAL
BONE FISH
SHRIMP
CONCH
YAMAHA
DAN
SOMETHING'S FISHY

A two-minute walk brings you to Tides Dive Center, situated on the lagoon en route to Turtle Inn's spa. The shop sells T-shirts and a few dive-related goods, and is extremely well-equipped – all you should bring is your own mask. Before diving, it's crucial to ask if there are any *pica pica* in the water. These are microscopic larval jellyfish, and if they're around, the shop's sunscreen-cum-repellent is a serious must-buy.

DIVE CENTER

The boats are all virtually new and designed to get you to the sites quickly. Although you are sheltered by the reef, the weather can pick up and the crossing can be a little bumpy. Take along a waterproof bag if you have a camera or anything else you want to keep dry.

The center's hookah breathing system allows non-divers to descend to a depth of 25ft; air is provided from a floating compressor. This is used at Laughingbird Cay and is an ideal stepping stone to becoming a qualified diver – something you can also do here.

The hotel beach is not of much interest for snorkellers unless there are manatees around or perfect visibility, so joining one of the dive trips is a must. The Cays are great for snorkelling, but what's really exceptional is the reality-adjusting whale shark dive or snorkel.

Most diving is organized as day trips, either to the inner atolls, thirty minutes away, or the barrier reef, an hour-long journey. With the exception of the whale shark dive, your surface interval is spent enjoying lunch on the white-sand beach of some palm-fringed, atom-sized island. The ever-smiling dive crew change your tanks while you indulge, and look after your gear at the end of the day. You don't have to lift a finger.

at a glance

Boats	26ft+ (wet, partially covered)
Group size	6
Instructors	2
Languages	English, Spanish
Courses	All PADI
Children	12+
Other	Computer and underwater camera hire, food and drinks, wash down, private charters, dive shop, hookah diving (helmet diving – no tanks, no experience necessary)

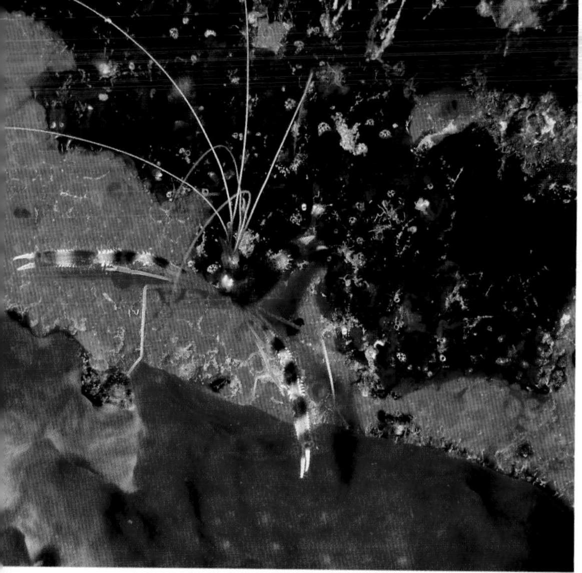

ABOVE
The attractive coral-banded shrimp is unfortunately a favourite for saltwater aquariums.

Many people go to northern and central Belize to dive, but what those areas offer cannot come close to the experience of diving Gladden Spit. A marine park since 2001 thanks to a groundbreaking initiative by Friends of Nature and the Belizean government, this is a site where, at the right time of year, diving or snorkelling with whale shark is virtually guaranteed.

DIVING

Whereas in the past Honduran fishermen would come to Gladden Spit to net the snapper that congregate here, nowadays the area is carefully monitored and protected in consultation with local dive operators. Boats are allotted a dedicated time slot to ensure that the whale sharks' natural behaviour is interrupted as little as possible, a policy that also offers a better experience for the diver. These are 'blue water' dives where you swim along at 60–70ft: the bottom is barely visible, and there is little to orientate yourself apart from the occasional dark shadow of a large bull shark or a blue marlin. If you come at the wrong time you may see nothing, but in the right season after the full moon, the diving here is literally unbelievable.

Fishermen always knew that something special was going on here: they regularly filled their small boats with a seemingly unending supply of line-caught snapper, and were constantly surrounded by whale shark. But it wasn't until a marine biologist came to dive that the link between the two species became clear. Enormous schools of snapper come here to spawn, producing billions of microscopic eggs that appear as great white clouds; this is what attracts the whale shark which come here to feed, their vast mouths agape. These gentle giants, up to 50ft long, will pass within inches of you; the first time you see one is an experience that stays with you forever.

at a glance

Local sites	12
Level	Easy to advanced
Visibility	50ft inside reef, 100ft outside reef
Must-dives	Gladden Spit, Glovers Reef
Snorkelling	Very good from dive boat
Wetsuits	3mm
Coral	Very good
Marine life	Whale shark, huge schools of snapper and jack, nassau, tiger, black and yellowfin grouper, sharptail eel, bull, nurse and lemon shark, loggerhead and leatherback turtle, bottlenose and spotted dolphin, Goliath grouper, manatee, toadfish
Other	Day trips, night dives, wreck dive, marine park

OPPOSITE, CLOCKWISE FROM TOP LEFT
The indigo hamlet is a common sight on the thriving reefs; diving with whale shark is a truly magical experience; an appealing honeycomb cowfish; a huge (and lazy) remora hitches a ride on a 40ft whale shark.

ABOVE
Large schools of jackfish are just one of the highlights of the blue-water whale shark dives.

LEFT
The central and southern Belizean reefs are home to a rich tapestry of marine life, including schools of sergeant major.

RIGHT
The loggerhead turtle is so slow-moving that it is always encrusted with marine growth.

ABOVE
Vast schools of spawning snapper rise from the depths – the moment that the whale shark have been waiting for.

RIGHT
The Belizean barrier reef is the second largest in the world, only exceeded by Australia's Great Barrier Reef.

Diving with whale shark is an incredible adventure, but while the experience cannot be exaggerated, this is not all that Belizean diving has to offer. Unlike northern Belize where the barrier reef hugs the coast off San Pedro, here it is some thirty miles away. In between lie various cays and atolls, where the corals are all in excellent health; visibility is somewhat limited compared to the barrier reef, but it's a true garden of soft waving fans.

Wall dives are the order of the day if you venture out to the barrier reef, the longest in the western hemisphere, which plummets here to 7,000ft. Fish life abounds: you will find moray, dolphin, nudibranchs, Goliath grouper, manta ray, eagle ray, bull and lemon shark. There are also four species of turtle, including the rarer, slothful loggerhead.

Laughing Bird Cay, half an hour away from Turtle Inn, is one of only three *faros* or submerged atolls in the world. The site of short day trips and night dives, it is home to two rare toadfish, the white-spotted and white-lined. It is also well known for inquisitive lemon and nurse shark. Glovers Reef is more spectacular, with walls falling to 2,000ft, although the trip requires calm seas. In short, this part of Belize will reward you with some truly amazing diving – surely the best in the Caribbean – and being in the water with whale shark is a true highlight.

Peter Island Resort
Deadman's
Beach Bar
and Grill

caribbean

Home to nearly forty island countries, the Caribbean has no shortage of desirable destinations, so it's odd that great hotels and great diving seem to be almost mutually exclusive. On the one hand, head south to the ABC islands (Aruba, Bonaire, Curaçao) or north to the Cayman Islands and you'll find some exceptional diving, but the accommodation is disappointing. On the other hand, travel to better-known places such as Antigua, Jamaica or Barbados and you'll stay at fantastic resorts, but the diving simply isn't up to scratch.

The British Virgin Islands give you the best of both worlds. It was Columbus who first put them on the map: he sailed through here in 1493 on his second visit to the New World, and named the untouched islands Las Virgenes in reference to Saint Ursula and her eleven thousand attendant virgins; such are the rights of discovery. Peter Island is at the epicentre of the area's wonderful dives, including the nineteenth-century RMS *Rhone*, widely recognized as the Caribbean's greatest wreck dive.

Step aboard the *Turks and Caicos Aggressor* II for something completely different: a snorkelling adventure with humpback whales, a truly life-changing experience. With the Turks and Caicos so near, it's also worth checking out Amanyara; located on the island of Providenciales, it offers that Caribbean rarity of fabulous diving combined with world-class accommodation.

Peter Island offers the perfect solution for diving in the Caribbean. Privately owned and almost impossibly large, comprising 1,800 pristine acres fringed with endless white-sand beaches, it is located right next door to the very best diving in the British Virgin Islands. The hotel first opened in the 1960s and gradually climbed its way upmarket. Today it has been revitalized as a true luxury resort.

peter island

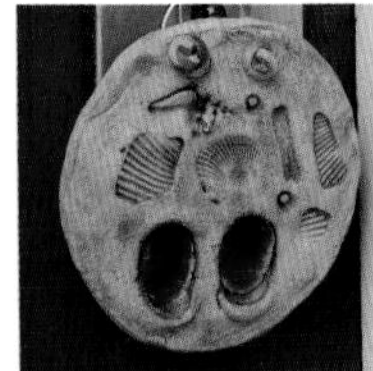

HOTEL peter island

Taming and running an island of this size is not cheap; just building the harbour was a major undertaking. It's a good example of how to make a small fortune by starting off with a large one. First bought by Norwegian millionaire Peter Smedwig in the late 1960s, Peter Island was taken over in the following decade by two entrepreneurs who lavished a veritable fortune on it. Like many private islands, this one ended up absorbing cash like a black hole absorbs light – unfortunate for the owners, but as a guest you get to reap the benefits.

You might expect the British Virgin Islands to be lush and verdant, but they lack the necessary rainfall. Peter Island is no different. A bit like a monk's head, it is thick with vegetation along its cultivated fringe, but this thins once you leave the shoreline. The manicured perfection of the perimeter is thanks to an army of gardeners and an all-encompassing irrigation system: together this creates a botanical dream, with all kinds of exotic palms, bougainvillea and frangipani crowding the carefully swept borders.

The resort sits next door to its own marina, which is also where the pool, restaurant and bar look out towards Tortola. Nearby are the thirty-two Ocean View rooms, which back onto the marina and offer glimpses of the sea through a screen of palms; the rooms

at a glance

Airport	Beef Island Tortola via San Juan
Airlines	American Airlines
Transfer time	35 mins by boat
Rooms	52 rooms, plus villas (all air-conditioned)
Staff ratio	4+
Activities	Watersports, basketball, golf (off island), fishing, swimming pool, hiking, tennis, gym, spa
Services	Internet, telephone, heliport, room service (breakfast and dinner)
Other	Mobile phones allowed
Children	8+
Power type	2-pin flat
Currency	US dollar
GMT	-5
Telephone	+284 4952000
Website	www.peterisland.com
Booking	www.diveinstyle.com

furthest away from the restaurant are the quietest, and also enjoy the best views. Their decor is American-Caribbean in style and fairly conservative, but they are nonetheless comfortable.

Your best bet for accommodation is a five-minute walk or a one-minute shuttle ride away. Here you'll find the twenty superb modern Beach Suites, which offer a generous sitting area, private terrace and vast bathroom with a spacious shower and bath for two. Better still, they give you captivating views over the ocean and neighbouring deserted islands, some opening onto an impeccably tended lawn, where you can relax in your own hammock.

In fact, the hammock is the emblem of Peter Island, and there are plenty more of them on the beach of Deadman's Bay. Nearly a mile long, it is a perfect white-powder crescent dotted with thatched huts and umbrellas. Unlike most beaches and bays in these islands, which tend to be crowded with charters, those on Peter Island are protected from uninvited guests; not only has the resort staked out its waters with buoys, but it has even gone to the extreme of setting aside a distant beach just for boats.

At the very end of Deadman's Beach is a truly world-class spa. Its unbeatable location overlooks a deserted white-sand cove, a favourite fishing spot for pelicans and home to what must be the finest snorkelling on the island. Even if you're not into spas, it's worth indulging in one of the excellent treatments just to gain access to the grounds. When you do, you can collapse into the hot tub and gaze out over the surf and the pelicans splashing in the shallows.

Until fairly recently, Peter Island had had the same chef for thirty years, surely a record for any hotel. New hands are in the kitchen but the food remains excellent, with international cuisine served at the open-air Deadman's Beach Grill and the air-conditioned Tradewinds Restaurant. The staff couldn't be friendlier, always stopping for a chat; you are treated more like a family friend than a hotel guest.

Peter Island is an upscale, manicured piece of the Caribbean. Not only does it keep getting better, but it has both the commitment and wherewithal to do so. Most importantly, while its design may not be as cutting-edge as at other resorts, its location is second to none.

mares

Diving at Peter Island could not be easier. Two minutes from any of the rooms and you are at Paradise Watersports, right on the private harbour and just yards from the dive boat. Thanks to the island's amazing location there is no need for painfully early starts; the wreck of the RMS *Rhone*, the British Virgin Islands' most popular dive site, is just fifteen minutes away, and you can depart at 9.30 a.m. after a delicious and leisurely breakfast.

DIVE CENTER

The small shop is stacked with equipment and even hires out digital underwater cameras. Although they prefer you to rig your own gear, all you have to do is ask and they will do this for you, as well as change your tanks for the second dive.

The boat is a wide, comfortable old 30ft cruiser, ideally suited to her task, especially since all the sites are under thirty minutes away so there is no need for day trips; once again, you can't beat Peter Island as a location for diving.

If you are lucky, you will get to dive with Randy, who owns the dive shop. His experience of these seas is vast, and not only will he regale you with stories of large shark encounters while working with film crews out in the deep, but you will benefit from his tremendous underwater knowledge: he seems to notice everything, and his enthusiasm turns even the most average dive into a treat.

Once you return to the island, you can just dump your gear and make a beeline for lunch. They will rinse and look after the equipment, returning it to the boat for the afternoon dive or the next day. This small, highly attentive dive team offers excellent, personalized service that complements the resort to perfection.

at a glance

Boats	30ft (dry, covered)
Group size	6+
Instructors	4
Languages	English
Courses	All PADI
Children	12+
Other	Computer and underwater camera hire, wash down, drinks, dive shop

ABOVE
The RMS *Rhone* has been underwater for 150 years and is now totally encrusted in thriving coral.

The Virgin Islands rank at the top of many dive magazine polls, especially in the USA, and it's easy to see why. The islands are easy to reach, the seas sheltered, the locals friendly, and the choice of resorts huge. What's more, the diving is truly excellent, including spectacular wreck dives. There is an abundance of fish life, and the variety of sites offers something for both novice and more experienced divers.

DIVING

The protected waters of the islands are ideal for snorkelling or diving. Snorkellers should head for the Baths at Virgin Gorda: a collection of giant granite boulders, these form a series of spectacular pools that are perfect for exploring. Weather permitting, it's possible for divers to venture to the outer reefs where there is a chance of encountering bigger life, from large schools of horse-eyed jack and African pompano to rainbow runner and permit. There are also sightings of shark, including bull, great hammerhead, lemon, and even silky, dusky and Galapagos shark.

The reefs are in great shape, with forests of waving fans and soft corals. There is also fire coral, especially at Santa Monica Rock; it stings, so keep your hands to yourself. The dives are mostly spur and groove reefs falling away to a sandy floor, often punctuated with blennies and jawfish, garden eels waving back and forth and large stingray that seem to think they look inconspicuous covered in sand; keep a look out in the turtle grass as, aside from trumpetfish, just occasionally you might see the beautiful golden-spotted snake eel.

What people really come here for, however, are the wrecks. The RMS *Rhone* is one of the world's most famous wreck dives, and you should probably dive her at least twice. Moored off Peter Island during the

ABOVE
Despite its vivid colours, the queen angelfish somehow blends into the reef.

FAR RIGHT
During the day you would hardly give a brain coral a second glance, but at night when feeding it becomes a thing of beauty.

MIDDLE
The thickly encrusted passenger deck of the *Rhone* provides a wonderful frame for viewing the marine life beyond.

RIGHT
After spawning, triggerfish are very territorial. Armed with a sharp set of teeth, they are known to nip unsuspecting divers.

at a glance

Local sites	25
Level	Easy to advanced
Visibility	100ft
Must-dives	RMS *Rhone*
Snorkelling	Good on house reef and from dive boat
Wetsuits	3mm
Coral	Very good
Marine life	Cobia, leopard and lettuce flatworm, eagle ray, gold-spotted snake eel, goldentail, viper, chain, spotted and green moray, reef, nurse, bull, great hammerhead, lemon and silky shark, humpback whale, tarpon, frogfish
Other	Night dives, wreck dives, marine park

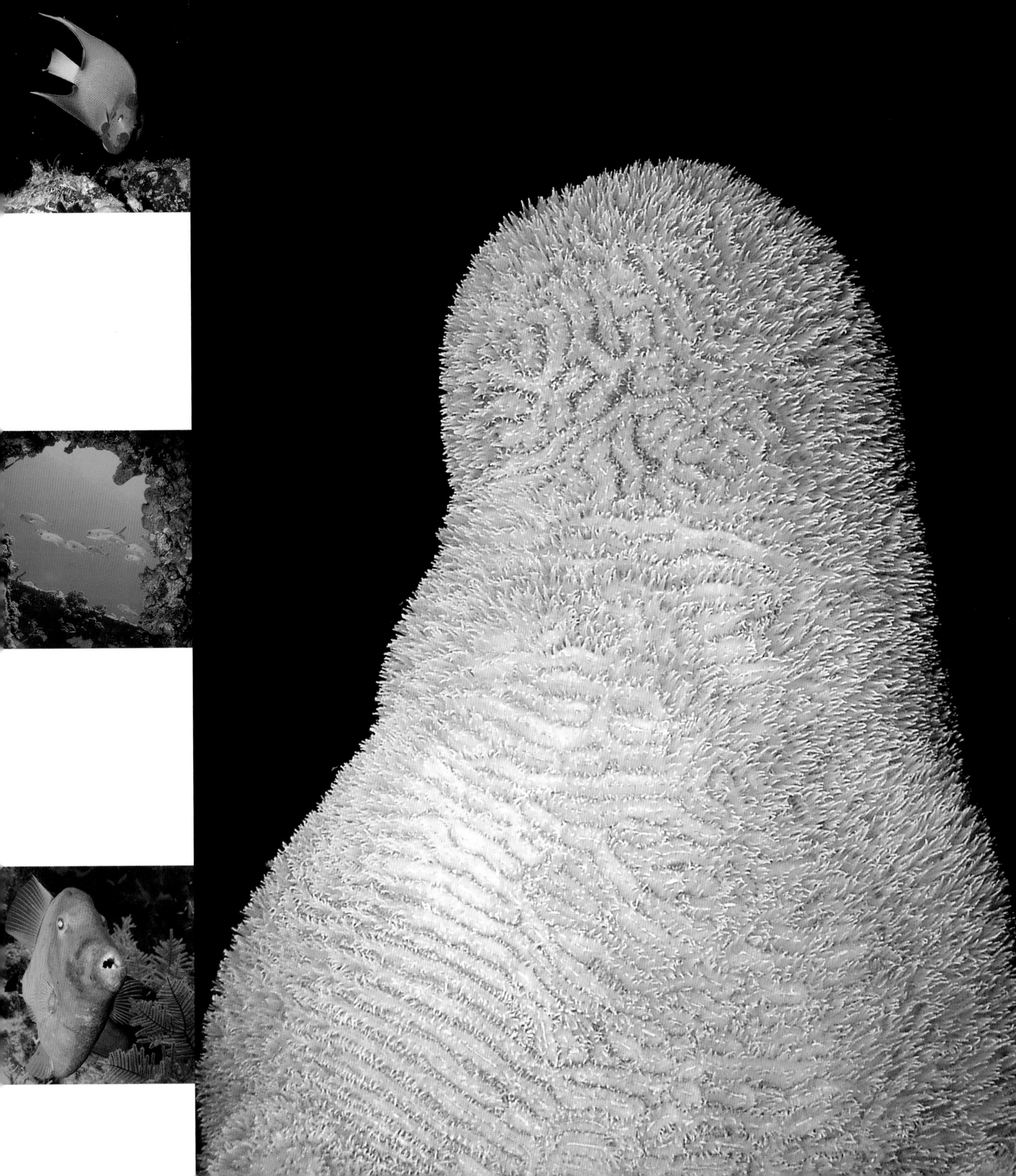

ABOVE

The RMS *Rhone* is considered the finest wreck dive in the Caribbean, and one of the best in the world.

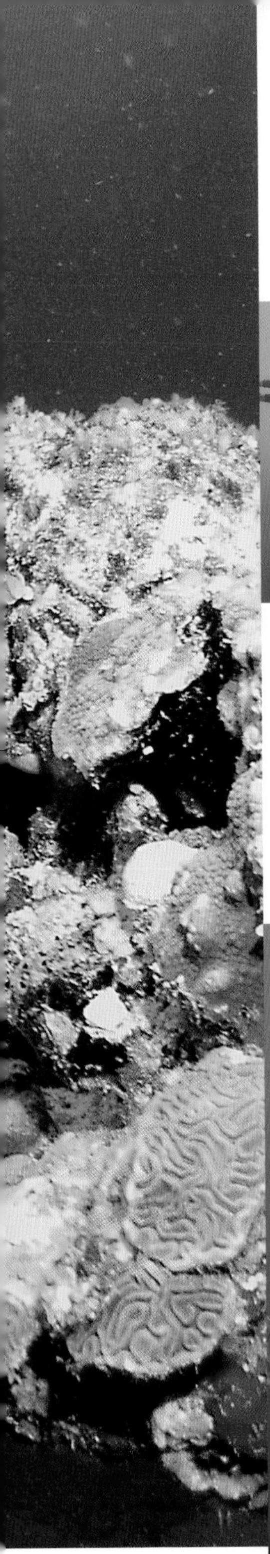

hurricane of 1867, she made a final dash to safety by heading for the open sea before sinking to the ocean floor just a few miles away. Today she is cloaked in corals and sits at a depth between 30–90ft; you usually tackle the deep bow first, then the shallow stern on your second dive. It is worth casting an eye over a plan of the wreck before diving (you'll find one on board the resort's boat), as this will help you make sense of what is scattered over the sea bed. There is much to see, including the honeymoon suite porthole, restored to glinting brass by divers rubbing for good luck.

The wreck has one major intact section, which was the setting of the 1977 film *The Deep*. You can comfortably swim inside, never losing sight of the blue open water. There is plenty of life, though you may have to search for some of it: yellow moray, lobster, barracuda, jack, grunt, soldierfish, spotted drum, queen angelfish, cowfish, octopus and green moray. Also check out the single remaining cannon, the ship's giant wrench set and the solitary anchor. This is a wonderful dive, full of marine life set against the haunting shapes of the ship enhanced by the filtered light of the sun, and you never know what you might come across in the endless recesses.

ABOVE
Spread across the ocean floor in three sections, the *Rhone* provides endless opportunities for exploring.

ABOVE
The *Rhone* is not the only wreck dive in the waters of Peter Island. This tugboat wreck is now captained by a turtle, which has taken control of the wheelhouse.

BELOW LEFT
As one of the earliest steel ships, the *Rhone* provides a solid base for 150 years of marine growth.

BELOW RIGHT
The clear waters around Peter Island offer an excellent diversity of coral life.

ABOVE

The sea grass is home to the rare and beautiful golden snake eel, as well as this more common trumpetfish.

LEFT

Hawksbill turtles are easy to find, but their young, with their pristine new shells, can be flighty.

ABOVE

The monochrome but striking juvenile drumfish is never still, even for a second.

LEFT

Convinced they are invisible, buried stingray can be approached within inches.

RIGHT

The thriving reefs close to Peter Island seem unaffected by El Niño.

ABOVE

Trumpetfish come in many shades, from from 'plain Jane' brown through vibrant yellow to this electric blue.

ABOVE

The reefs harbour masses of spiny lobster. This slipper lobster is a more unusual sight.

LEFT

Angelfish come in some amazing colours and patterns.

It all seems faintly surreal. Sitting in a hot tub on the stern of a 120ft boat, far from land and in the middle of the warm waters of the Caribbean, you behold all around the spectacle of humpback whales breaching, tail-slapping or just swimming by lazily with their newborn calves. Just a glimpse of such activity would be thrilling witnessed from a cold, rain-lashed, whale-watching boat – here it soon becomes the norm.

BOAT turks and caicos aggressor II

The *Turks and Caicos Aggressor II* is a 120ft dive boat. Built in 2003, she normally plies the waters of the Turks and Caicos islands, but for just six weeks a year she steers a few hundred miles off course to the Silver Banks, south of the Dominican Republic. Here you can enjoy the extraordinary experience of getting up close and personal with 40 tonnes of humpback whale. An eight-hour haul from Puerto Plata deposits you midway between the Dominican Republic and the Turks and Caicos islands in the northern Caribbean – it's quite a way, so bring along sea-sickness medication just in case. Once you set anchor, however, you are protected from the ocean swell by an enormous horseshoe reef, so you can put your pills away and relax.

There are berths to suit a range of budgets. The fully air-conditioned cabins come as quads, doubles or a more spacious stateroom. The quads are ideal for families, while the doubles are suitable for couples; note that cabins 8 and 9 are closest to the constantly-running generator. The solitary stateroom is set in the bow and offers a larger bed and a bit more room. Storage space is generally limited, but wetsuits and snorkel gear are all stored on the covered dive deck so there is just enough room to hang your things. Luckily you can definitely pack light as the boat is deeply informal and you're bound not to use all your clothes.

at a glance

Airport	Puerto Plata
Airlines	American Airlines, Continental Airlines
Transfer time	30 mins by car
Cabins	9 (all air-conditioned)
Staff ratio	1
Services	Email, DVD player, jacuzzi, digital cameras for hire, email, satellite phone
Children	10+
Power type	2-pin flat
Currency	US dollar
GMT	-5
Telephone	+649 2310404
Website	www.aggressor.com
Booking	www.diveinstyle.com

Construction of the boat took two years, overseen by the watchful eye of captain–owner Piers van der Walt, and no detail has been overlooked. Each cabin has a wall-mounted DVD player, and there is an up-to-date selection of over two hundred films to choose from. Email accounts are set up on boarding and there's even a satellite telephone available, so you're never out of touch – unless, that is, you want to be. Short informative 'whale lectures' and slideshows after dinner help you understand what you are witnessing, but if your attention ever strays, you can just look out the window and see it happening right in front of you.

You spend just five days out on the Silver Banks, with two daily outings on rigid inflatables. After breakfast you're given a thorough briefing from Piers, and then you're off in search of that special encounter. Spending two three-hour sessions on a small rubber boat under the hot sun may sound trying, but as soon as the action starts, any discomfort is swiftly forgotten.

When you leave you are offered a DVD featuring footage shot during your stay. At US$60, it does not come cheap, but it does serve as a wonderful reminder of your adventure; it almost makes you wish you'd left your camera at home and instead focused on enjoying the moment. If you prefer to take your own shots, however, you can choose from an extensive range of digital and 35mm underwater cameras to hire.

The quality of the food varies. Breakfast sets you up for the day with porridge, eggs and pancakes, while lunch is normally some kind of pasta, warmingly welcome after hours either in the water or in a damp wetsuit. Dinner is less satisfying as there is a shortage of fresh ingredients on board; it may be worth asking in advance whether the boat can stock up with *mahi mahi* at Puerto Plata.

All in all, there is no safer or more comfortable way to experience swimming with humpback whales. After an incredible day in the water with these wonderful creatures, you return to a hot tub, cocktail and movie in bed. It doesn't get much better than this.

Every year, from late January to late March, huge numbers of humpback whales brave the 1,500 mile journey from the north Atlantic to the warm sheltered waters of the Silver Banks, close to the windsurfing mecca of the Dominican Republic. For reasons still unknown to science, they travel here to give birth to their 12ft calves, mate again, and then turn back for the long haul north. During this 3,000-mile round trip, they never feed.

ABOVE
This could be you, swimming just a few feet away from forty tonnes of trusting humpback whale.

SNORKELLING

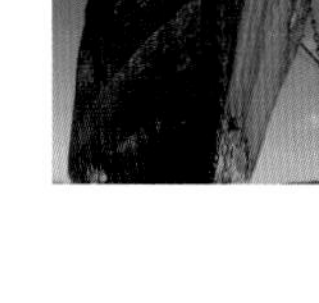

This is a trip where there is no need for the typical 'expect to see' briefing. At the right time of year, the underwater action is guaranteed. You *will* swim with 40ft-long, 40-tonne whales and their calves; you *will* witness their massive breaches and tail slaps; and, if you're lucky, you may even enjoy the company of an inquisitive juvenile or 'Valentine'. These encounters – where you float on the surface and let the whales come to you, and not the other way round – can put you within an arm's length of these magnificent creatures.

Nothing quite prepares you for the first time you slip into the water, mask and snorkel on, and find yourself hovering above a fully mature, sleeping behemoth. Even though you are completely safe, it's impossible to keep your heart from racing; you are torn between fear and wonder. It is quite simply a privilege to be in the water with these amazing mammals, especially when you consider that despite being hunted by man, they are one of the few animals that will allow you to come between them and their newborn offspring.

The best thing is, you need no qualifications to enjoy this incredible experience. If you can snorkel, you can swim literally within inches of some of nature's biggest and greatest stars, and you will come away with memories to last a lifetime. It is truly magical.

OPPOSITE TOP
Humpback whales aren't all there is to see. It is quite common to come across schools of dolphin, which seem to enjoy interacting with man in these remote waters.

OPPOSITE MIDDLE
From tail slaps to breaches, you will encounter the whole spectrum of the humpback's vocabulary.

OPPOSITE BOTTOM
The whales are so close you could touch them. Normally the mother remains in deeper water, casting a watchful eye as her calf rises to greet you.

at a glance

Local sites	12
Level	Easy
Visibility	50–80ft
Snorkelling	Unbelievable
Wetsuits	3mm
Coral	Poor
Marine life	Humpback whale, spotted dolphin, nudibranchs
Other	Marine park

Just to the south of Corsica in the western Mediterranean, the Italian island of Sardinia is a mountainous slab of granite blessed with endless white-sand coves, and offers some of the best diving in the Mediterranean. In 1960 the Aga Khan led a group of investors in buying some thirty-five miles of its most stunning coastline, and proceeded to transform it into what is now known as the Costa Smeralda or the Emerald Coast, named after the distinctive colour of the island's surrounding waters.

To many, the Costa Smeralda is Sardinia. Much of its appeal today is thanks to its developers' foresight in imposing strict controls on building and careful protection of the natural environment. Thus, even after over forty years of development, the place still seems relatively unspoilt, and new restrictions on building on the coast mean it's likely to stay that way.

Sardinia is quiet for most of the year, but things heat up in July and August, when the sun shines at its brightest and the beautiful people arrive in droves. For a six-week period, luxury yachts moor in the bays while their owners relax in the picturesque town of Porto Cervo and party at the appropriately named Billionaire's Club. Prices rocket due to the incredible demand, and many resorts stay open for just four months. Still, the reason people keep coming here is the promise of tranquillity, and Hotel Pitrizza gives you just that.

Tucked behind its own private beach on a small granite headland, Pitrizza occupies a prime position on Sardinia's wild but exclusive shoreline. First opened in 1963 and substantially refurbished in 1990, its design is in keeping with the rest of the Costa Smeralda: nature has been respected, and the grounds and architecture are in perfect harmony with the rugged landscape of Sardinia's northeastern coast.

sardinia

HOTEL pitrizza

The rustic, mostly single-storey stone buildings blend into the background so well that they are reminiscent of hobbit-dwellings, albeit incredibly stylish ones. The swathes of bright green grass that link them to the beach also run up and over them – it's common to see gardeners mowing the lawn, perched on the roof.

Pitrizza's fifty-five rooms are scattered across the grounds in small clusters. Understated in design, they feature white-plastered walls accented by local tiles and furniture, including a king-sized bed. A panoramic sheet of glass separates your bedroom from the terrace, so you can enjoy the view even with the windows closed. But would you want to? The air is saturated with the sweet, gentle scent of jasmine, a welcome perfume that wafts into your room. If this isn't reason enough to switch off the air-conditioning, most people leave their windows open just for the sound of the lapping sea, which you can hear from anywhere in the resort.

The rooms are connected by a network of terracotta brick-tiled paths that wind through the hotel's olive trees, bougainvillea, roses, hibiscus and oleander. Many of them overlook the Med, and these naturally command a premium; if you want the very best, go for a room west of the main clubhouse. Even more upscale (and with

at a glance

Airport	Olbia
Airlines	Easyjet, Meridiana
Transfer time	30 mins by taxi
Rooms	55 villas (all air-conditioned)
Staff ratio	2+
Activities	Watersports, golf, tennis, squash, horse-riding, fishing, go-karting, spa, swimming pool, gym
Services	Internet, telephone, television, DVD player, room service
Other	Mobile phones
Children	All ages
Power type	2-pin round
Currency	Euro
GMT	+1
Telephone	+39 0789 930111
Website	www.starwoodhotels.com
Booking	www.diveinstyle.com

more space) are the hotel's fifteen suites. And if those aren't good enough, then there is always a whitewashed villa with its own tiny private beach, or else up on the Capa di Sopra, high above the rest of the complex, you can choose between two hilltop villas that come complete with private pools.

At the heart of the hotel is a bar and an indoor–outdoor dining area with views to the beach; sky-blue cane furniture and vivid red geraniums adorn the wide terracotta-tiled terrace, from which you can take in the azure and emerald waters below. Bamboo umbrellas and navy-blue-clad loungers dot the coarse sand, set along a series of small intimate coves.

In true Italian style, dining tends to be alfresco, looking out over the signature saltwater infinity pool; hewn out of granite, this is a sort of giant rockpool with much of the stone left in its original state. Given that it relies on the sun for heating, it is always refreshing. Food is included in the hotel rate for a relatively modest supplement – this offers excellent value, as in return you'll get a combination of style, service and superb Italian cuisine (including some fantastic *gelati*). If you fancy a change, you can eat at any of the other hotels belonging to the Starwood group – Cervo, Cala di Volpe and Romazzino – at no extra cost. But excellent as these are, none come close to Pitrizza.

Pitrizza is only open from May to September, a season of just four months; the water is too cold to swim in at any other time of year, as currents from the Atlantic pour in through the narrow Straits of Gibraltar. As a guest, you benefit from the fact that during the rest of the year, its owners are working behind the scenes to ensure that all is utter perfection for 'the season'. Sure, there's a price to pay – as the temperature soars, so do hotel rates all over the Costa Smeralda – but you'll be staying in what is by all accounts the finest hotel in the Mediterranean, which also happens to have access to some of the region's best and most varied diving. In Europe, diving in style doesn't get much better than this.

650

Proteus Diving is an easy five-minute drive from Hotel Pitrizza, and a private charter will pick you up from the hotel's beach if you request it. You generally have to look after your own gear so it's easiest to rent theirs, but this isn't a problem; you get excellent and personalized service from the small, friendly team. Most importantly, you will only ever dive with five in your group (some local centers lead dives that number in the twenties).

DIVE CENTER

The boat is a 20ft Zodiac with a powerful outboard and is excellent for travelling to the sites, most of which are reached within thirty minutes over the protected and usually calm waters. There are fifteen other dive operators on the Costa Smeralda so the sea may look a bit too busy for comfort, but don't worry – there are about forty dive sites, so underwater crowds are never an issue.

Like the hotel, the diving season is dependent on the weather and lasts from May to September. The water can be chilly early on but reaches a relatively balmy 25°C (roughly 75°F) at the peak of summer; June is a good month to come, but September is possibly the best as the sea is still warm but the crowds will have disappeared. The center has wetsuits for all conditions (offering double 5mm protection in May), but as always it's best to bring your own mask and, in this instance, a hooded vest. Combine this with their equipment, and even the colder months shouldn't be an issue.

Dives take place either in the morning or the afternoon. It's all very civilized and personal, with no jarringly early starts and normally just one dive per trip. Private charters offer the most flexibility and you can even take a two-tank dive, enjoying your surface interval with lunch on one of the small white-sand beaches on the coastline.

at a glance

Boats	20ft Zodiac (wet, open)
Group size	5
Instructors	2
Languages	English, Italian, Spanish
Courses	All PADI, CMAS
Children	14+
Other	Computer hire, food and drinks, private charters, nitrox, rebreathers
Website	www.proteusdiving.it

ABOVE

Diving the dramatic canyons and passages of this coastline is an almost architectural experience.

Diving in Sardinia offers aquarium-like conditions with almost limitless visibility. Often described as the most exciting diving in the Mediterranean, it is both varied and suitable for all divers, from novices to the more experienced.

DIVING

A major reason why the diving is so good is that this corner of Sardinia is actually a national park, La Maddelena. You'll come across more fish life here than anywhere else in the Med; at Picchi di Punta Coticcio, for instance, there are moray, octopus, large grouper, beautiful nudibranchs, scorpionfish, lobster and schools of castagnole, creating a scene reminiscent of the Red Sea. There is not much big life at any of the sites, but you can find a large group of good-sized groupers to the north in the islands of Lavezzi, which seem totally unfazed by divers' paparazzi-like behaviour.

The most spectacular aspect of the diving is the underwater landscape. Sardinia's islands are made of granite, with rock formations reminiscent of the Seychelles sliding into the depths. Secche dei Monarci, a pair of underwater pinnacles, is renowned for its vivid red gorgonian corals, while Grotta di San Francesco is an experience in itself: after being greeted by a grouper known as the Receptionist, you enter a tunnel to emerge in a clear aquamarine pool, open to the skies and framed by overhanging rock. Soaring granite walls, canyons, gulleys, caves and current-swept peaks provide a stunning backdrop for any dive, and the remarkable range of sea life in this so-called dead sea is just the icing on the cake.

at a glance

Local sites	15
Level	Easy to advanced
Visibility	100ft
Must-dives	Punta del Papa, Lavezzi
Snorkelling	None
Wetsuits	5mm+
Coral	None
Marine life	Grouper, Mediterranean moray, octopus, scorpionfish, conger eel, nudibranchs, schools of barracuda, electric ray, red gorgonians
Other	Day trips, night dives, marine park

OPPOSITE, CLOCKWISE FROM TOP LEFT

This is probably the only place in Italy where you can see calamari not on a plate; large groupers have made a comeback in this marine park and are relatively approachable, especially at Lavezzi; moray eels and conger eels inhabit the craggy walls; surprisingly beautiful scorpionfish swim in these waters, their perfectly camouflaged colours revealed only by the camera's flash.

egypt

Egypt's Sinai Peninsula is a triangular wedge of raw shimmering desert jutting down into the Red Sea and like many deserts is topographically stunning. But here the contrast of red sand running into clear blue water is especially striking. Almost at the tip of this arrowhead lies Sharm el-Sheikh, perfectly placed to access the world-renowned dive sites of Ras Mohammed National Park and the Straits of Tiran.

Once a sleepy fishing village, Sharm used to be the only settlement on this desolate yet dramatic stretch of the Red Sea, and as recently as 1982 there was only one place to stay. Things have moved on in recent years, and while the town is still backed by arid hills and *wadis* rolling out of the desert, today it hosts some 138 hotels either completed or under construction. Most of them cater to tourists on cheaper package holidays, but this shouldn't have any impact on your stay. Just head straight to the Four Seasons – of all the hotels, this oasis of a resort stands head and shoulders above the rest.

The only land bridge between the two continents of Africa and Asia, Sinai borders Israel to the north and faces Saudi Arabia across the Gulf of Aqaba to the east. While the peninsula's strategic significance has made it synonymous with a troubled past, visitors should not be put off coming here. If there are risks, then they are unlikely to be greater than those of modern living anywhere in the world.

A few years ago the site of the Four Seasons was simply desert – breathtaking and dramatic, but nonetheless just sand and rock. Now, thanks to the miracles of desalination, it has been transformed into a verdant oasis. Opened in 2002, the resort's grounds tumble down a gentle incline to the shores of the Red Sea, some three hundred mature palms marking the stark boundary between the hotel's lush gardens and the arid surrounding landscape.

HOTEL four seasons sharm el-sheikh

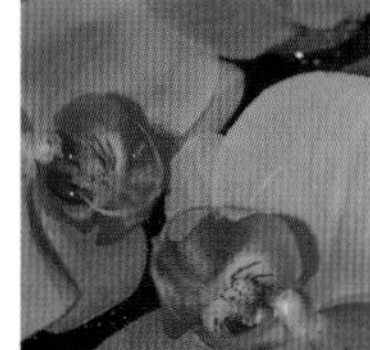

A broad drive leads you to the hub of the hotel, a spacious structure clad in cream stone and defined by Egyptian architectural detailing. Here you will find the reception and a number of restaurants, which look out over the grounds to the water below. To the north of this are the 64 two-bedroom suites, ideal for familes, while to the south lie the other 136 guest rooms.

Despite offering more than two hundred rooms, this is not a place that crowds you. The lush gardens are broken up by small, bougainvillea-strewn piazzas on different levels, reached by either wide stone paths or an electric tram (a child's delight). These unique spaces lend the resort the feel of a small village. You rarely see the complex as a whole; instead, you are continually moving from one beautifully landscaped area to another.

All rooms have their own private terraces, some of which give directly onto the gardens or, for a premium, offer lofty views of the land falling away to the sea below. The marble-floored interiors are simple yet elegant, and at the end of the day provide a cool, quiet haven, complete with incredibly comfortable bed – a Four Seasons trademark – fluffy pillows, delicious duvet and (naturally) Egyptian cotton sheets, changed daily. The bathrooms are just as luxurious.

at a glance

Airport	Sharm el-Sheikh direct or via Cairo
Airlines	British Airways, Egypt Air, Monarch
Transfer time	10 mins by limousine
Rooms	210 (all air-conditioned)
Staff ratio	4
Activities	St Catherine's Monastery, Bedouin camp, desert quad biking and horseriding, coloured canyon trip, swimming pools, spa, gym
Services	Telephone, television, internet, DVD and CD player, room service
Other	Mobile phones
Children	All ages
Power type	2-pin round
Currency	Egyptian pound, US dollar
GMT	+2
Telephone	+69 3603555
Website	www.fourseasons.com
Booking	www.diveinstyle.com

TO GET BACK
MY YOUTH I
WOULD DO
ANYTING IN THE
WORLD EXCEPT
TAKE EXERCISE
GET UP EARLY OR
BE RESPECTABLE.

The architects did a superb job, but it is the landscapers who have really triumphed. They have planted no fewer than 1,800 palms, and in a land where water is at a premium, no courtyard is short of a trickling fountain. A stream flows down a series of rock-strewn beds from the heart of the hotel, and the soothing sound of moving water blends intoxicatingly with the scent of jasmine and the colours of the vegetation.

You can choose to eat down at the beach or up at the main building. The Reef Grill, perched on a small bluff above the sand, offers fabulous views of the island of Tiran and is perfect for a simple lunch or light dinner. Up at the hotel itself, you can dine at the Moroccan–Lebanese restaurant Arabesque, or at Il Frantoio for Italian cuisine alfresco. The food is excellent, if on the expensive side, so you may want to load up on the delicious and extensive breakfast, included in the room rate.

Although none of the hotels on Sinai's coastline has a world-class beach, the Four Seasons has made the most of its own red-sand crescent with an array of carefully positioned private niches, which give the impression of seclusion even when the beach is full. You can swim directly off the shore, but it's best to grab your mask and fins and walk to the end of a jetty, where you can drop into some 15ft of water and snorkel with lionfish.

The staff are exceptional: welcoming, friendly and keen to help in whatever way they can. They do a first-class job at looking after children, but if you'd rather avoid the kids, steer clear of the resort at the end of October when many schools are on holiday.

If you want a change from diving or snorkelling, there is plenty to keep you busy. Facing the water, it is easy to forget the beauty of the desert behind you, where you can do everything from quad-biking to paying homage to St Catherine's Monastery at the base of Mount Sinai.

The Four Seasons is not a small hotel, but feels much smaller than it is. If you're after truly guaranteed sunshine, wonderful diving, superb friendly service and a luxurious, impeccably managed resort with local flavour, look no further.

Sinai Blues is located at the core of the Four Seasons' beach, not more than five minutes from any of the rooms. This highly professional operation offers both dive trips and snorkelling excursions, and a truly extensive range of gear is available to hire. There are never more than six divers to an instructor, so you can count on enjoying individual attention both on the boat and underwater.

DIVE CENTER

The Red Sea is very heavily dived, and the Egyptian government has stepped in to limit the number of dive boats in its waters. Although this is capped at three hundred, including live-aboards, many vessels find their way to Sharm, so don't be surprised by the armada of white hulls crowding the horizon.

The secret to avoiding all this is to wind your body clock a few hours forward. If you are going south to Ras Mohammed, it's best to leave the dock by 7 a.m.; you won't be back until early afternoon, so order a packed breakfast and lunch basket before you set out. If you are heading north to the Straits of Tiran, then an even earlier start of 6 a.m. is advisable; once you've enjoyed some solitary diving, the fast Rib will return you to the hotel in time for the amazing breakfast.

Sinai Blues' fleet is managed by the delightful Riham. A high-speed rigid inflatable will take you to the Straits in under fifteen minutes, while a larger motorboat will transport you to the more distant sites of Ras Mohammed. The crew more than live up to the Egyptian reputation for hospitality, looking after your gear, rinsing it for you, and helping you in and out of the water. Despite heavy demand at peak times, the dive center never loses its personal touch, and with nine instructors to hand, this is a great place to learn to dive.

at a glance

Boats	28ft+ (wet open, dry covered)
Group size	6
Instructors	9
Languages	English, Arabic, French, German, Italian, Japanese, Spanish, Dutch
Courses	All PADI
Children	8–10 for Bubblemaker course, 10+ for open-water certificate
Other	Computer hire, nitrox on request, food and drinks if ordered in advance, private charters, gear prep and wash down
Website	www.sinaiblues.com

ABOVE
Lionfish are in abundance at the end of the Four Seasons' jetty, ideal for snorkellers and divers.

The Red Sea has some wonderful diving, and despite its popularity, Sharm el-Sheikh still offers some of the best. This is mainly thanks to its location, right at the point where the Red Sea splits into the Gulfs of Suez and Aqaba. In addition, there is a plethora of diveable wrecks along Egypt's coastline.

DIVING

Some argue that the ultimate diving in the Red Sea is only to be found on a live-aboard ploughing its way either to the Brother Islands or to Sudan and the far south. However, around Sharm you can find examples of virtually every known coral species in this body of water, together with nearly as many fish species as there are on Australia's Great Barrier Reef.

Most of the diving is done at two locations: the Straits of Tiran just to the north, and the Ras Mohammed National Park to the south. Ras Mohammed is the place most people have heard about, but don't forget Tiran, which is just as rewarding and also happens to be more conveniently located. There are well over thirty-five immediate sites to choose from, so you could easily spend a week here without diving the same spot twice.

The topography of the reefs varies from gentle slopes to full walls. The one thing they all have in common is that the top is always just a few feet beneath the surface, ensuring that not a second of your time underwater is wasted; your safety stop is as good as the rest of the dive. This also means the reefs are fantastic for snorkellers, who can even join the dive trips to Ras Mohammed. Closer to home, the hotel beach rewards snorkellers with schools of lionfish and

at a glance

Local sites	35
Level	Easy to advanced
Visibility	100ft+
Must-dives	Small Crack, Shark Reef, Yolanda Reef, Jackson Reef
Snorkelling	Very good on house reef, excellent from dive boat
Wetsuits	7mm December–April, 5mm May–June, 3mm July–September, 5mm October–November
Coral	Excellent
Marine life	Schooling hammerhead, jack and barracuda, silky, grey reef, leopard and whale shark, Napoleon wrasse, crocodilefish, bottlenose dolphin, manta and eagle ray, giant moray
Other	Day trips, night dives, wreck dives, marine park, hyperbaric chamber in Sharm el-Sheikh

ABOVE
A member of the sea urchin family, devoid of its normal array of spines, is easy prey for triggerfish and pufferfish.

OPPOSITE TOP
Red Sea bannerfish are often found in pairs or larger schools.

OPPOSITE MIDDLE
Night dives are the only time you will ever find a stationary parrotfish. For once, you can appreciate their beautiful colourings at your leisure.

OPPOSITE BOTTOM
Geometric morays are one of three types frequently found in the Red Sea. Giant morays can easily measure over 9ft long.

OPPOSITE MAIN PICTURE
Relaxed hawksbill turtles are a common sight, especially in the Straits of Tiran.

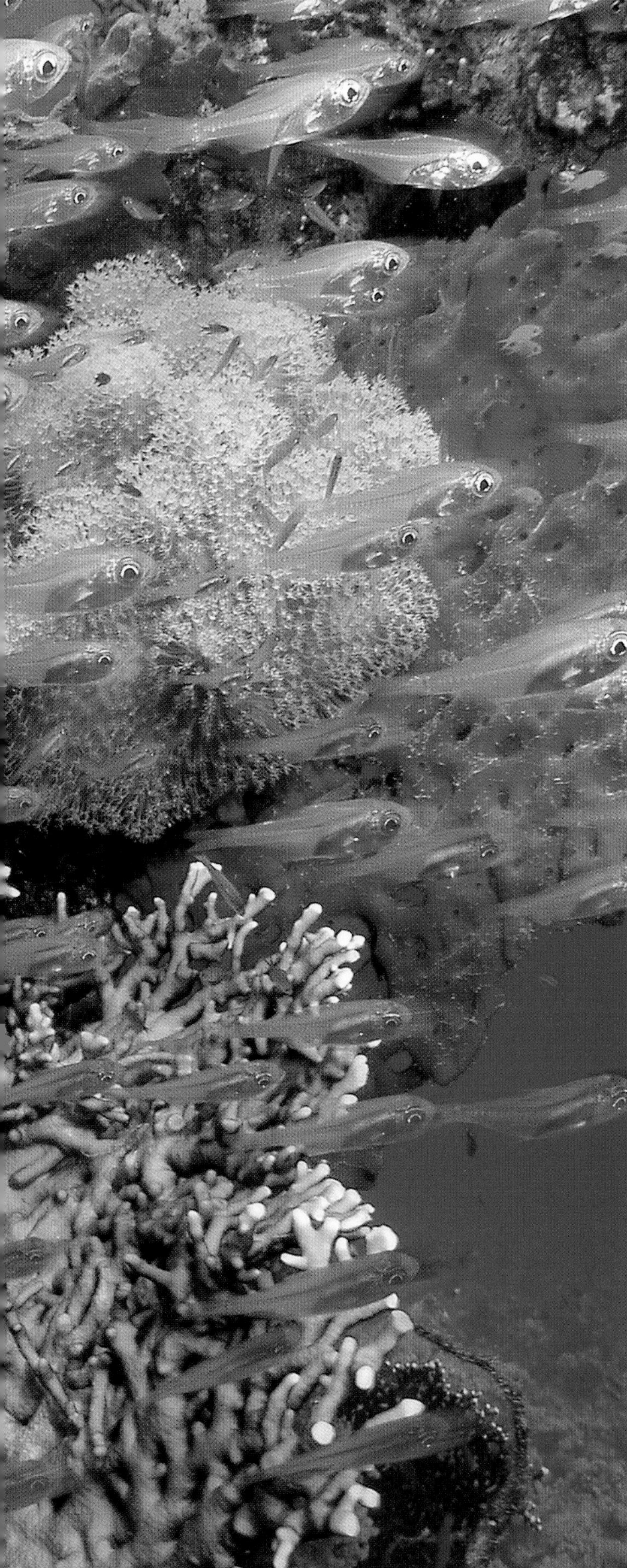

LEFT
There is literally a blizzard of life on most of the Red Sea's reefs. Despite over-diving, it is both plentiful and in excellent health.

even a resident crocodilefish, while those who want to learn to dive can do no better than here, there being no real current to speak of.

Both hard and soft corals abound and are in excellent health. An amazing diversity of sea life inhabits them, ranging from the distinctive technicolour anthias to schools of hammerhead, jack and barracuda, in the summer months. Giant green moray are present on every dive, and they live up to their name: it's not unheard of to find a relaxed 9ft eel fully exposed on the coral, some with truly vast heads.

One of Sharm's most outstanding dives and snorkels is at Small Crack, right at the tip of the Sinai Peninsula. In the right conditions, you start out on the outer edge of the reef where there is a chance to see leopard shark and schools of barracuda and jack. Within Small Crack itself, the variety of life is spectacular, and since it's very shallow there is no need for a torch as all the colours are incredibly vivid. It's the nearest thing to a flooded florist's.

The Red Sea has a number of wreck dives. The *Thistlegorm* is the most famous and requires an early start as it is quite distant and often crowded. You'll love it if your fantasy happens to be sitting astride a sunken 1940 BSA motorbike or swimming among Bren-gun carriers, though otherwise you may find it disappointing it as the sea life here is nothing special.

There are simply too many sites to describe, let alone recommend, as they each have their day; what you will see is really a matter of luck, the season and your instructor's knowledge. If you can bear the heat, the best time to dive the Red Sea is probably midsummer, as this brings schooling fish and shark. Nonetheless, whenever you visit, be sure to get an early start and you will be richly rewarded.

LEFT
Anthia, the signature fish of the Red Sea, are found in abundance dancing over the reefs.

OPPOSITE
With up to 150ft visibility, the Red Sea's pristine reefs are home to well over a thousand species of fish and over two hundred types of coral. It is not just the breadth of marine life, from tiny glassfish to giant whale shark, but also the sheer quantity that makes this such a great area to dive.

tanzania

Tanzania was born when the republics of Tanganyika and Zanzibar came together in 1964. Home to Mount Kilimanjaro, Africa's highest mountain, this east African nation is the site of one of the world's largest migrations of wild animals, including wildebeest, zebras and gazelles. Though today it is economically poor, its past is incredibly rich, and the most fascinating of its history belongs to Zanzibar.

Once the capital of Oman, one of the wealthiest nations in Africa, Zanzibar has long been known as the Spice Island. Its past is littered with slave traders and colonists, and even now it is a byword for the exotic. The city of Stone Town is definitely worth a visit; the chances are you will pass through here if you're heading to any of the nearby islands. The place to stay is the Serena Inn, right on the beach. It's the perfect base for wandering the city's streets and markets, and provided your room fronts the ocean, you can watch the *dhows* return from sea against the setting sun. Dinner on the roof of the Emerson and Green Hotel is also a must, but be sure to book in advance.

Just to the north of Zanzibar is the lush, verdant island of Pemba, home to a huge variety of tropical fruits and herbs, as well as endless clove plantations – the air is saturated with their sweet, spicy scent. Hidden away on the coast is Fundu Lagoon. There is no road access so the only way to get here is by private boat, but once you step onto dry land it's like a being different world – one nestled on an expanse of white powder.

Hidden away on the west coast of Pemba Island, this hotel was carved out of the jungle by a group led by enterprising British fashion designer Ellis Flyte. In 2001 they stumbled on the location almost by mistake, and they then took a gamble on an unknown South African architect for the design. The risk has paid off: the result is a truly unique resort.

pemba

HOTEL fundu lagoon

It took just twelve months to transform this place from virgin forest into fully functioning hotel. The construction was no doubt sped up by the owners' hands-on approach: they monitored every step, and even today they spend over half the year running and fine-tuning their creation. Virtually everything is locally built using materials native to the area. This is not the polished, detailed handiwork you would see on the roof of a Fijian buré, but the roughly finished craft you might expect on a safari stay in a Tanzanian village.

Don't be fooled by rustic appearances: you'll find all the creature comforts you need. But what makes this place special is that you never forget where you are. It is all incredibly laid-back and informal, with a strong vein of Africa running throughout: African head carvings, masks and other original items collected on the owners' travels. If this weren't enough to remind you of your location, the families of friendly monkeys and nocturnal bushbabies will do the job for you – just remember not to leave your sunglasses out overnight as they may not be there in the morning!

A long, handcrafted jetty stretches out into the lagoon, branching off to an overwater bar; you'll need to travel its length to access the deeper water, a better place for swimming than the beach.

at a glance

Airport	Zanzibar via Dar es Salaam, Nairobi or Johannesburg
Airlines	British Airways, Emirates, KLM, South African Airways
Transfer time	45 mins by taxi then 20 mins by boat
Rooms	16+
Staff ratio	3+
Activities	Canoeing, nature walks, forest trips, catamaran charters, dhow cruises, dhow fishing, yoga platform, limited spa, pool table
Services	Television in Activities Room
Other	Mobile phones
Children	12+
Power type	3-pin square
Currency	Tanzanian shilling, US dollar
GMT	+3
Telephone	+255 242232926
Website	www.fundulagoon.com
Booking	www.diveinstyle.com

A fine powder-sand path leads to the beachside rooms; an irregular stairway to the hillside ones. The latter offer extra privacy and wonderful views, and, open to the trade winds, help keep you cool – a bonus if the ceiling fans aren't enough for you. Every room is essentially a tent – a large, airy African tent swathed in mosquito netting, set on a raised wooden platform and sheltered by a soaring traditional thatched roof. It is, if you like, a tent within a house. The bed faces directly out over the fabulous view, and the canvas panels fold back to give access to the spacious south-facing timber deck.

Aside from diving, there isn't a huge amount to do here; chilling out is the order of the day. If you want a break from the beach, the small spa offers delicious treatments based on perfumed local apothecary oils. The canoes, wakeboards and waterskis hanging in the dive shop hint at more energetic pursuits, but demand for them is low, particularly as there is no proper tow boat.

Still, it's worth summoning up the energy for a day trip: divers and snorkellers alike will be rewarded by a visit to nearby Mesali, a marine sanctuary with amazing snorkelling, a fine white-powder beach and excellent swimming in the clear turquoise waters. Or you can take out a 30ft catamaran for a day's sailing and explore the beautiful beaches scattered in the area around Pemba.

Breakfast and dinner are served in the main restaurant overlooking the beach, but lunch is something of a treat at the overwater bar. The food is simple but always well prepared, based on local ingredients including freshly caught fish. The service is attentive if a little slow, but then again, people don't come here for the hectic pace of city life.

Most of Fundu's staff are drawn from the small local village; they are incredibly friendly, and everywhere you go you are greeted with '*Jambo*' ('Hi' in Swahili). This is one of the few places where a hotel has really been able to do something for the community. It took a bit of work at first to convince the locals that building a hotel would be a good idea, but the village has been rewarded with improved conditions, including better building materials and the foundation of a new school, all courtesy of the hotel.

Fundu is a different kind of resort. Simple yet stylish, it offers real charm and character – and grows on you at an alarming rate. As the owner's quest to perfect her dream continues, including plans for a pool, the allure of this remote, roughly hewn jewel can only intensify.

PLEASE CHANGE BED LINEN

Just off the jetty of Fundu Lagoon, this incredibly well-run dive center is the focus of all the resort's water-based activities. Whether you want to snorkel, dive or spend a day on a deserted beach, this operation will make your dreams come true. While the center is quite large – there is a schoolroom and freshwater rinse-down tank – the groups are kept small, and it's up to you to set your own pace.

DIVE CENTER

The center offers an excellent range of gear, from Scubapro regulators to Mares BCs in all shapes and sizes, though children are not specifically catered for. Your fins and mask are kept in a bag marked with a name tag so there is little chance of losing them.

The yellow-hulled boats are sturdy, fast 20ft Rigid Raiders, powered by a pair of outboards. They offer no protection from sun or weather and are only really suited to shorter journeys, so for the full-day 'safaris' be sure to bring an extra towel to sit on. However, they do nudge right up to the shoreline, so access to the boat is not difficult.

Depending on the tide, you reach the boat either by a short walk or a longer trek to the end of the jetty. There are always drinks on board, while a full lunch is provided on the day trips; at Mesali you'll eat under the shade of simple thatch, while on the north and south safaris your meal will be served on a deserted white beach.

The diving here is highly personalized and brilliantly organized. There is little for you to do, and at the end of the day all you have to do is dump your equipment on the boat and head straight for that warm shower. The dive team will then transport your gear to the center, where they will rinse and dry it, ready for your next dive.

at a glance

Boats	20ft Rigid Raiders (wet, open)
Group size	6
Instructors	2
Languages	English
Courses	All PADI
Children	14+
Other	Computer hire, food and drinks, gear prep and wash down

ABOVE
Many species of ray inhabit the waters off Mesali Island, including this large marble ray.

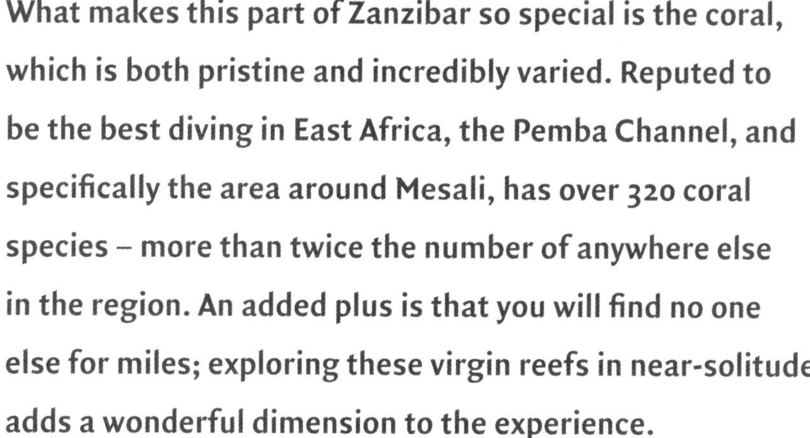

What makes this part of Zanzibar so special is the coral, which is both pristine and incredibly varied. Reputed to be the best diving in East Africa, the Pemba Channel, and specifically the area around Mesali, has over 320 coral species – more than twice the number of anywhere else in the region. An added plus is that you will find no one else for miles; exploring these virgin reefs in near-solitude adds a wonderful dimension to the experience.

DIVING

Visibility varies, ranging from about 60ft to over 100ft, and to get the most out of diving here you really need to dive on an incoming tide. This will offer you the best visibility and the highest chance of encountering the big pelagics that frequent these waters. When you book your holiday it's worth checking with the dive center that you will be able to do at least some of your diving in these conditions.

You can opt to go on a day-trip 'safari' north or south of Pemba, with lunch on a deserted white-sand beach; if you venture south to the Wreck, be sure to go via the Emerald Lagoon, which will reward you with turquoise waters, low-lying sandbanks and tranquil dhows. However, most dives are around Mesali, a beautiful white-sand island base a short boat ride from the hotel, and all the sites are no more than five minutes away. Entry is by backward roll, and there is usually time for dive groups to gather on the surface before descending.

A common starting point is Apartment, a comfortable, easy dive centred around a coral bommie rising to some 40ft; the top is just 20ft below the surface. This is a hive of activity, literally littered with morays, ranging from the giant green moray to the rarer whitemouth. You'll also find their black-cheeked brother, the most aggressive of the otherwise largely docile family.

at a glance

Local sites	12
Level	Easy to advanced
Visibility	60–100ft+
Must-dives	Mapanduzi
Snorkelling	Excellent from dive boat
Wetsuits	3mm
Coral	Superb
Marine life	Honeycomb, giant green and whitemouth moray, hammerhead shark, devil ray, eagle ray, torpedo ray, Napoleon wrasse, schooling barracuda, schooling unicornfish, giant grouper, bumphead parrotfish, cowrie
Other	Day trips, night dives, wreck dive

RIGHT
A school of bannerfish, a dramatic contrast against the clear blue waters.

RIGHT

A school of chevron barracuda feeding in the strong currents of Mapanduzi.

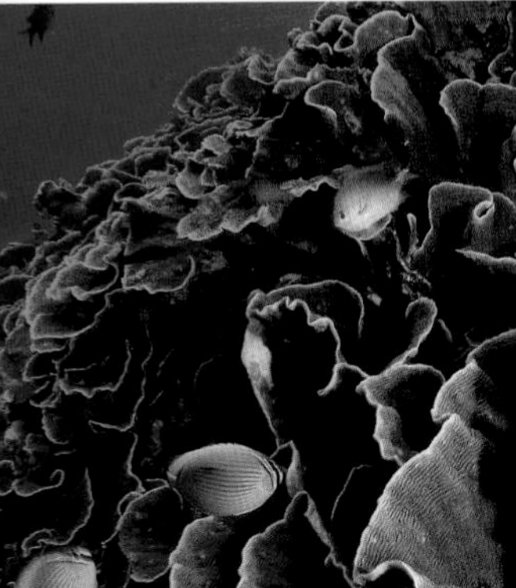

ABOVE

All kinds of fish find a perfect hiding place in the acres of pristine cabbage coral.

Coral Gardens is a gentle dive, perfect for poking under ledges and investigating various nooks and crannies; these conceal an abundance of ray, but watch out for torpedo ray, capable of delivering a stunning electric shock. There are also lionfish, nudibranchs, schools of chubb, octopus, and all the usual range of tropical fish. Be prepared to exercise your buoyancy skills as the rocks are festooned with beautiful sea urchins, with their alien-like blue patterns and symmetrical spotting.

BELOW

Danger, high voltage: the torpedo ray delivers an electric shock to immobilize its prey. It can also do the same to divers who are tempted to touch.

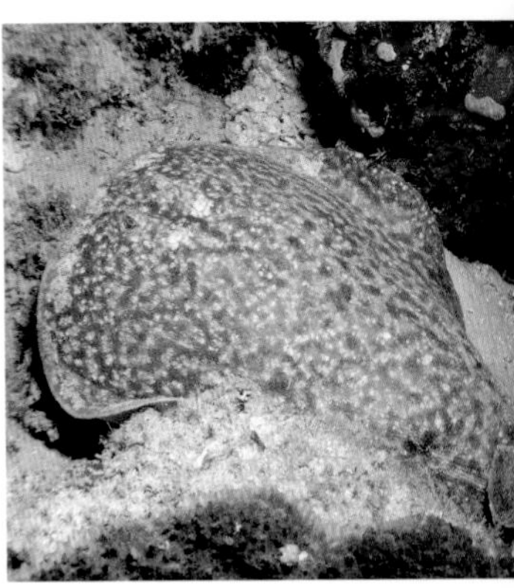

OPPOSITE, CLOCKWISE FROM TOP LEFT

Regal angelfish, one of the most beautiful inhabitants of the reef, are never found far from shelter; the reefs are peppered with flatworms, which come in a variety of striking patterns; beautiful flatworms prove that nature's colours can never clash; the amazing hues on the undersides of feeding anemones are only revealed by artificial light.

If you manage to dive on an incoming tide, Mapanduzi is the main event. A gentle wall with a deeper drop-off, it goes down to over 100ft before tumbling into the abyss (which means over 1000ft). You need to descend fast as it only really comes to life when the strong currents kick in. These can bring in anything from a school of hammerheads or giant barracuda, to a family of eagle ray or inquisitive Napoleon wrasse.

Pemba is still relatively uncharted territory, but it has plenty to offer: marine life of all sizes, acres of coral, an untouched environment, and some brilliantly organized diving. Now is the time to come.

mozambique

Mozambique is a nation with a turbulent history. Located at the crossroads between the Middle East and India on the southeastern coast of Africa, it was once a trading port for gold, ivory and slaves. Its fortunes took a turn for the worse in the last century: the former Portuguese colony gained independence in 1975, but was officially one of the poorest nations on earth. A period of socialist mismanagement and fifteen-year civil war did little to help, with peace finally coming only in 1992.

One of the few positive outcomes of all this is that Mozambique is still relatively untouched – and it is certainly unspoilt by tourism. Yet this beautiful country has plenty to offer visitors: a stunning, completely undeveloped coastline, amazing colonial architecture and some of the friendliest people in Africa.

Foreign investment is on the rise, led by two pathfinding luxury island retreats, Quilálea and Marlin Lodge. Both lie just off the Mozambique coast, with Quilálea in the Quirimbas Archipelago to the north and Marlin Lodge in the Bazaruto Archipelago to the south. Separated from one another by a thousand miles, they offer very different tastes of the country, not to mention the diving. But they have one thing in common: both destinations are so untouched that you'll have the ocean all to yourself.

Quilálea literally means 'retreat', and nowhere is this term more appropriate. Tucked away in the Quirimbas archipelago on the northernmost edge of Mozambique, this outpost of luxury is remote by any standards. The island has hosted a local population for years, originally drawn here by its lack of fresh water. That may sound odd, until you realize that this means there are no mosquitoes, and therefore no malaria.

quilálea island

HOTEL quilálea

Getting here is not exactly straightforward. The jumping-off spot is the town of Pemba (not to be confused with Pemba Island in Tanzania), which you reach via Johannesburg or Dar es Salaam. From there, you take either a two-and-a-half-hour jeep trip followed by a thirty-minute boat run, or – a far better option – a twenty-minute charter to the neighbouring island of Quirimbas. After a five-minute drive and a short wade out to a small catamaran, you finally have Quilálea in your sights. If your map isn't enough to indicate that you are on a bit of an adventure, then by now you will have got the point. A recent alternative to this is the direct helicopter transfer.

Only the northern end of this eighty-six-acre island has been tamed; the rest is in its virgin state, and the surrounding waters are both a marine park and World Heritage site. There are just nine rooms, spread out over the colourfully planted gardens filled with the chatter of birds. Perched on low cliff-tops or opening directly onto the beaches, the villas are built of local materials, with high thatched roofs and plain plastered walls. A king-sized bed draped in netting takes centre stage indoors, while outside is a shady terrace from which you can enjoy a private, unobstructed view over the lagoon. The lodgings are simple but extremely comfortable, though avoid room 3, situated a little too close to the generator for comfort.

at a glance

Airport	Pemba via Dar es Salaam or Johannesburg
Airlines	British Airways to Dar es Salaam, British Airways or South African Airways to Johannesburg, Mozambique Airlines to Pemba
Transfer time	20 mins by plane then 10 mins by boat, or 20 mins by helicopter direct (inclusive for 7-night stays)
Rooms	9 (all air-conditioned)
Staff ratio	5
Activities	Swimming pool, canoeing, island tours, deep-sea fishing, massages
Services	Television in bar
Children	12+
Power type	2-pin round
Currency	Mozambican metical (US dollar and South African rand accepted)
GMT	+2
Telephone	+258 272 21808
Website	www.quilalea.com
Booking	www.diveinstyle.com

At the core of the resort is a protected cove, flanked on either side by the open-sided bar and restaurant. Unlike southern Mozambique where perfect white-sand beaches are the norm, here crushed coral and seashells line the water's edge. Still, the beach is pretty enough, but bear in mind that it is not ideal for swimming as the sea bed is peppered with small coral heads.

Don't expect the trappings of a traditional five-star hotel – the real attraction of Quilálea lies in the sheer get-away-from-it-all factor. A natural haven, the island is an avian paradise, and you're bound to see – and hear – a plethora of exotic birds: bee-eaters swoop from tree to tree, African sea eagles soar majestically overhead, and the most startling but elusive kingfisher offers brief glimpses of its incredible plumage. Another natural highlight is Mahat, a wet-nosed bushbuck that wanders the island and will often join you for dinner on the beach, drawn by your table's flower arrangement, which she will proceed to eat.

Aside from fishing and diving, chilling out is the order of the day. A carved totem of healing hands marks the way to the esoteric treatment room overlooking the main beach, where you can listen to the sound of the sea below while you have a massage – it's worth scheduling one for high tide. Alternatively, you can cool off in the small saltwater pool, or if you're feeling energetic, follow the island path to see baobab trees in flower, nesting sea eagles and, if you're lucky, turtles – you can take breaks at any of the deserted beaches en route. Those struck by island fever can hop to nearby Ibo Island to see an untouched part of Africa, or relax on a sunset cruise aboard the hotel's traditional *dhow* or sailboat.

Breakfast and lunch are normally in the restaurant or by the pool, but you can also dine on the beach under a carpet of stars. The food is fresh, simple and delicious: the focal point for most meals is locally caught fish and seafood, cooked to perfection by the always smiling Nathan.

Quilálea is an eco-resort with a unique charm; everything has been crafted by locals and you never forget where you are. The pace of life is zero, and you've probably gathered by now that the dress code is incredibly relaxed. In fact, there doesn't seem to be one, and since laundry service is included in the bill, this is one far-off destination you can really pack light for.

Like the rest of the resort, the small dive center is charmingly rustic: bundles of confiscated local fishermen's spear guns, masks and fins adorn the walls – this is a marine park, after all. There are no other divers for miles, and because groups are kept to a maximum of four people per dive, you really get a sense of being alone on an adventure.

DIVE CENTER

Boarding is from the beach – a pair of wet shoes come in handy here. The boats are two small but quick 17ft catamarans and a larger converted fishing vessel, the *Sencar*. There is no shade on the smaller boats, but given the proximity of the sites, this is really not an issue; the *Sencar* does have shade but is that much slower. All are fine for the sites dived at present, but if the center plans to do day trips in future, they may need something more purpose-built.

Because the seas surrounding Quilálea are largely uncharted, a lot of underwater potential has yet to be unlocked; they have only just dipped their toes into these waters when it comes to discovering what is here, let alone what there might be. It's therefore crucial that you have a top-class guide who knows the sites and has had time to do a bit of exploring, so do make sure that the resident instructors have been in place for a few months before you arrive – you will need them to tap into the best the area has to offer.

Quilálea offers inclusive packages, and although drinks and most major activities are excluded, diving is covered for a small supplement of US$30 a day – it's certainly the cheapest diving I've ever done.

at a glance

Boats	17ft+ (wet open, dry covered)
Group size	4
Instructors	2
Languages	English
Courses	All PADI
Children	12+
Other	Computer hire, drinks, gear prep and wash down

ABOVE
Unlike nudibranchs, flatworms have no exposed gills, but they are just as beautiful.

Around Quilálea are some sixty miles of St Lazarus Bank, home to some of the world's best unexplored diving. It can be a bit hit and miss: when you hit, you encounter 8ft-long turtles, but when you miss, you're still guaranteed world-class nudibranchs and some unusual life forms – hardly a compromise. The island has almost unique access to all of this, so you can be sure of one thing: you won't be bumping into any other divers.

DIVING

New dive sites are being opened all the time. There are currently nine within easy reach – although in reality there must be ninety, just waiting to be discovered. Three of these are must-dives: Casino, Estadia Da Luz, and surprisingly enough, the house reef, Lagosta Alley. The latter is the easiest and suitable for beginners, while the former need a more experienced hand. Visibility was disappointing during my visit – even if you avoid the rainy season, it's difficult to predict how clear the water will be – but you can tell from guests' photographs that it is usually a lot better.

What is lost in water clarity at Casino is made up for in marine life. Going down to about 90ft, the reef system is more of a series of shelves than anything else, and it is along here that life congregates. Even with 40ft visibility, it's possible to spot bull sharks, giant green turtles and morays, Napoleon wrasses and huge schools of batfish. There's also an amazing variety of nudibranchs and flatworms; it's not that unusual to come across new species. Other visitors include spinner and bottlenose dolphin, white-tip reef shark, giant loggerhead turtle, kingfish, barracuda and guitarfish.

For the intrepid, there are some seriously fast drift dives. The speed of the current sweeping you along the walls of soft coral doesn't

at a glance

Local sites	9
Level	Intermediate to advanced
Visibility	50ft
Must-dives	Casino, Estadia Da Luz, Lagosta Alley
Snorkelling	Average on house reef
Wetsuits	3mm
Coral	Good
Marine life	Ocellated lionfish, nudibranch, spinner and bottlenose dolphin, manatee (dugong), ribbon eel, giant green turtle, bull shark, giant potato bass, Napoleon wrasse, white-tip reef shark, guitarfish
Other	Marine park, night dives, hyperbaric chamber in Johannesburg (2.5 hrs)

OPPOSITE RIGHT, ABOVE
If you want to see unbeatable nudibranchs, look no further than the waters around Quilálea.

OPPOSITE RIGHT, BELOW
The rare and relatively unknown ocellated lionfish has made the house reef its home.

OPPOSITE LEFT, TOP TO BOTTOM
Leaf scorpionfish come in a variety of colours; the blue ribbon eel morphs from black to blue then finally to yellow as it changes sex from male to female; it may be hard to believe, but leaf scorpionfish are difficult to see without a strong light.

LEFT
A typically oversized Quilálean nudibranch weaves a winding ribbon of eggs.

BELOW
Leaf scorpionfish rely on camouflage to protect themselves from predators. That doesn't explain why some are bright pink...

give you time to linger, but you do get a chance to see bull shark and a family of three enormous grouper: two are big by any standard, while one is a true Goliath – about the size of a Volkswagen Beetle.

This kind of adventure diving is truly exciting, and although many sites are for the more experienced, there are also easier ones. Lagosta Alley can be reached from the beach and you are guaranteed to see ribbon eel, rare ocellated lionfish, a pair of red- and green-leaf scorpionfish, mantis shrimp, even more stunning flatworms and nudibranchs (up to six inches long), painted lobster and blue-spotted stingray. Though it begins unpromisingly, this is probably one of the best house-reef dives around.

This is great diving. You can choose from very fast drifts to more protected sites, and what you will see tends to be of a size beyond belief. Quilálea is not a snorkelling destination – you definitely need to dive – but coming here is an adventure in itself.

LEFT

Longnose hawkfish are a treat to see. Most are solitary, but sometimes they form pairs.

RIGHT

Relatively plain by day, leopard cowries exhibit a beautiful mantle at night.

BELOW

Once your eyes get used to spotting them, you'll see stunning nudibranchs everywhere.

There are just two hotels on Benguerra Island's twenty square miles, and the one that occupies the prime position on the west coast is Marlin Lodge. Built in 1995, it was originally the fishing lodge of a wealthy South African enthusiast who was drawn by the unparalleled game fishing in the surrounding waters. Where fishermen lead, divers often follow, and from these humble beginnings, the lodge has reinvented itself as a fully fledged boutique resort.

benguerra island

HOTEL marlin lodge

Creating accommodation like this in such a remote location is a feat in itself. The owner has shown remarkable far-sightedness – what with Mozambique's wonderful coastline and new-found stability, further resorts will not be long in arriving. Benguerra is not a private island, and this is no bad thing: unlike many sanitized, fenced-off resorts, Marlin Lodge is very much a part of the local scene. Fishermen visit to trade their catch, the occasional local wanders the beach balancing a bundle on their head, and traditional dhows drift past in the gentle wind.

There are just nineteen rooms, spread along a berm of sand just behind the beach. All overlook the ocean and are reached by a timber walkway raised above the local flora and fauna, which gives you both a cool breeze and views of the island. A handful, known as Classic Chalets, date back to the resort's origins and offer good value for money. The walls and roofs are thatched with local reeds, and the interiors are simple but charmingly furnished with a four-poster bed, stylish lamps and beautiful bed linen.

The rest of the rooms are made up of the newly designed Luxury Chalets and Executive Suites, which range from very comfortable to utterly luxurious; the suites are basically upscale versions of the

at a glance

Airport	Vilanculos via Johannesburg
Airlines	British Airways, South African Airways or Virgin Airways to Johannesburg, then Pelican Air to Vilanculos
Transfer time	7 mins by bus then 25 mins by boat
Rooms	19 (some air-conditioned)
Staff ratio	3+
Activities	Swimming pool, fishing, village tours, island picnics, walks, sunset cruise, full range of watersports
Services	Wellness Centre
Children	All ages
Power type	3-pin round
Currency	Mozambican metical (US dollar and South African rand accepted)
GMT	+2
Telephone	+27 12 5432134
Website	www.marlinlodge.co.za
Booking	www.diveinstyle.com

18+19

Do Not
DISTURB

chalets, with larger bathrooms and both indoor and outdoor showers. The interior walls are clad in a light beige fabric that emphasizes the feeling of space, while a four-poster bed draped in mosquito netting is perfectly positioned to give you the best views over the shady deck and the ocean beyond. Although more could be made of these vistas – perhaps by trimming back some of the trees and shrubs – care has been taken to ensure that the buildings blend into their natural setting and provide total privacy. Do note, though, that rooms 1 and 2 may be a bit too close to the main hub of the hotel.

The reception, bar and restaurant are housed in interconnected structures with a soaring reed-thatched roof. They offer a compelling combination of modern Western and traditional Mozambican elements: polished timber floors, honey-coloured timber railings, a bamboo-clad bar, and deep, comfy sofas for lounging and taking in the sights of the pool and sea. The restaurant lets you dine in both the shade and the open air, but every few days you will find the furniture missing, transported to the beach for a barbecue around a roaring bonfire. Unsurprisingly, the menu is built around fish (a set menu offers alternatives), and the food is served by smiling, attentive and mostly local staff. A waiter is assigned to you throughout your stay, so help is never far from hand.

Most guests seem to spend their time either by the pool or on the beautiful white-sand beach. For the horizontally inclined, the beachside Wellness Centre offers beauty treatments and also a limited range of massages. Adventure-seekers can take advantage of the truly amazing fishing; there is also a Hobie Cat and a full range of watersports available, although the more leisurely inclined might prefer a sunset cruise. Pansy Island, just north of Benguerra and named for the pansy shells or sand dollars that wash up on its giant sand banks, is the perfect spot for lunch or a break between snorkelling or diving; en route you can visit a flock of flamingos or, if fortune favours you, you might spot a few humpbacks or dolphins.

Marlin Lodge is something of a triumph in a country that until just a few years ago was riven by civil war. Things are only going to get better. As it stands, there is no more comfortable or stylish way to enjoy the wonders of the beautiful and remote Bazaruto Archipelago.

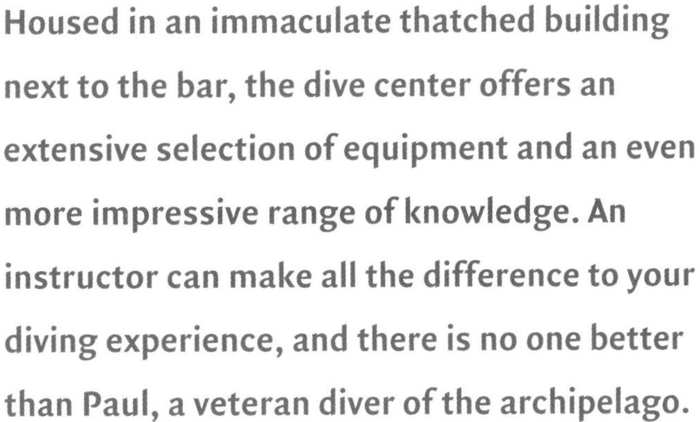

Housed in an immaculate thatched building next to the bar, the dive center offers an extensive selection of equipment and an even more impressive range of knowledge. An instructor can make all the difference to your diving experience, and there is no one better than Paul, a veteran diver of the archipelago.

DIVE CENTER

Since there is just one guide, groups can be as large as the maximum of eight. Nonetheless, groups of three or four are common as the majority of guests come here for the deep-sea fishing, which is reputed to be the best in the East Indian Ocean.

As with virtually every destination in this book, your gear is taken care of until the end of your stay. It can be a bit of a walk to the boat when the tide is out, but this is no great hardship when you're treading on soft white sand carrying only your towel and, at worst, your dive computer.

There is an extensive range of diving vessels, from a purpose-built high-speed open boat to a fleet of modern, shady catamarans. This gives you a choice of speed, ideal for nearer sites, or comfort, excellent for day trips or going further afield.

One of the great advantages of diving at Marlin is that snorkellers can join many of the trips. Divers can venture outside of Two-Mile Reef while snorkellers stay within it; they can then meet at Pansy Island, a huge sandbar surrounded by turquoise waters and calm inlets, and a great place to picnic or while away a surface interval.

at a glance

Boats	21ft+ (wet covered, dry covered)
Group size	8
Instructors	1
Languages	English
Courses	All PADI
Children	12+ (smallest size XS)
Other	Food and drinks, gear prep and wash down, private charters

ABOVE
There is a wide variety of incredibly cute, colourful but reclusive boxfish.

This is unspoilt diving at its very best. The Bazaruto Archipelago is protected as a national park: there is no large-scale fishing here, just sport-fishing outside the boundaries. Thus the reefs are exceptionally healthy, particularly the soft corals, and the range of sea life is not only vast but also remarkably approachable.

DIVING

at a glance

Local sites	12
Level	Easy to advanced
Visibility	50ft+
Must-dives	Cabo San Sebastian, Two-Mile Reef
Snorkelling	Very good from dive boat
Wetsuits	3mm (5mm May–August)
Coral	Good, especially soft
Marine life	Whale shark, devil ray, manta ray, honeycomb moray, loggerhead, green and hawksbill turtle, guinea-fowl moray, large nurse shark, kingfish, barracuda, giant potato grouper, hammerhead, eggshell cowrie, schooling surgeonfish, schooling bannerfish
Other	Marine park, night dives, day trips, hyperbaric chamber in Durban (2 hrs)

About halfway between the two major islands of Bazaruto and Benguerra lies Two-Mile Reef, the main local dive site for Marlin Lodge. The sheltered side is excellent for snorkelling, while the ocean side offers some fantastic diving. The ocean floor is fairly shallow, maxing out at roughly 65ft, so long dives are an option. Due to the reef's length and Paul's expertise, you can always find part of it to dive, practically regardless of currents – not that they're particularly strong to begin with.

Visibility averaged at around just 50ft when I dived, but what could be seen was still impressive. The gently descending seabed provides hundreds of caves and gullies, some of which conceal 11ft nurse shark (worthy of an entire Discovery Channel documentary) as well as white-tip shark. The flood tide can bring clear water along with enormous schools of barracuda, trevally and the occasional kingfish, but there is always an endless procession of tropical fish, set against a soft-coral reef background reminiscent of an underwater flower stall.

Honeycombs, the most passive of morays, are plentiful; some giant ones seem to know Paul and will accept a scratch. There are also schools of orange-spined surgeonfish hanging around coral heads,

RIGHT
The beautiful blue-spotted stingray is a common resident of Benguerra's waters.

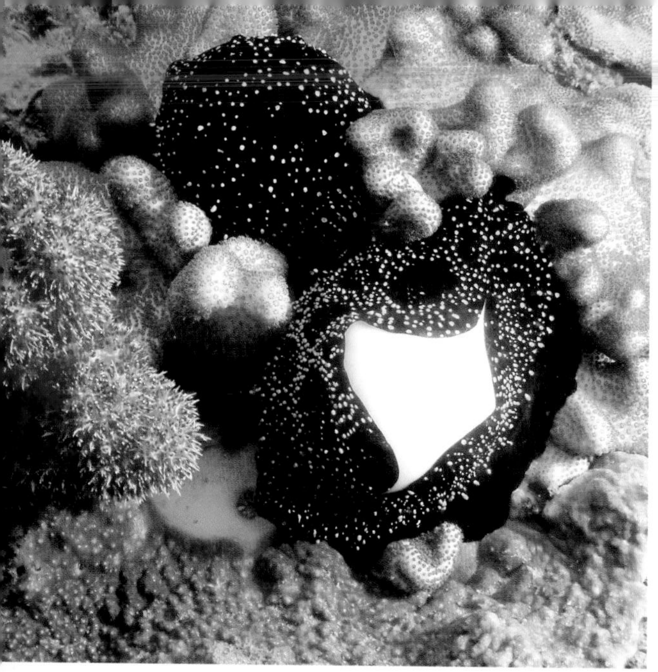

LEFT
It is becoming difficult to find large, living shells anywhere in the world, but stunning eggshell cowries abound in Mozambique. Their black mantles are a striking contrast to their white shells.

ABOVE
The bizarre but beautiful sea apple, a type of nudibranch, looks similar to a cardinal's hat.

ABOVE
The docile honeycomb moray is a common sight.

various nudibranchs including the amazing sea apple, crocodilefish, congregations of eggshell cowries, lionfish, swarms of glassfish, boxfish, white-spotted porcupinefish, blue-spotted ray, guineafowl moray, hawksbill, green and loggerhead turtle, carpets of anemones and their Nemos... the list goes on. And, during summer from November to March, you're bound to encounter the elusive whale shark, which arrive in droves along with manta and devil ray.

More experienced divers can go to Cabo San Sebastian, a fisherman's paradise that starts at 100ft. Well over an hour from the lodge, it can only be found with the help of GPS, and while gearing up you can see the waters churn around you with schools of game fish. There is no distinct reef edge here, more like a gently descending current-swept plain, partially forested by green tree corals. Every now and then, the plain is broken by shallow gullies that hold sea life hiding out of reach of the current; it's wonderful to behold all manner of life slowly revealing itself, from lionfish and 3ft-long potato cod to grey reef shark, hammerhead and huge turtles.

The surface interval is just as rewarding. I spent mine trawling under the stewardship of professional fisherman Jonathan, whose every move seems like a ballet. In no time at all, I worked my way up from plastic bait to a large yellowfin tuna, which promptly became sashimi at the bar.

BELOW
There is no shortage of sea life in the Bazaruto Archipelago.

ABOVE

Bannerfish rarely travel alone. Usually they swim in pairs or schools.

BELOW

Small, soft corals literally cloak the reef like a flower stall.

RIGHT

Relaxed schools of orange-spined surgeonfish populate the many coral outcrops.

Seychelles

A thousand miles off the coast of east Africa en route to nowhere, the Seychelles are one of the most pristine and scenically stunning places on earth. They offer a rare blend of topographic beauty, stylish hotels and delicious cuisine; mix this with great diving and you have an irresistible cocktail. Even the most enticing brochures fail to do this far-flung archipelago justice, with its white beaches, crystalline waters and striking boulder formations, all set against a backdrop of lush vegetation.

The Seychellois government realizes how much this politically stable republic has to offer, but also how little – tourism is its lifeblood, and the nation depends on it to survive. The Seychelles' fragile natural beauty is their most powerful drawcard, and the authorities have fully faced up to the need to protect it. There are strict controls on new hotels and almost fifty per cent of the islands' land mass has been designated as nature reserves and national parks; luckily for divers, no less attention has been paid underwater. In this far-sighted way, the country is continuing to attract the visitors it needs while ensuring that tourism will never get out of hand.

The Seychelles comprise 115 white-lipped atolls and islands spread over almost a million square miles. Mahé is where you land, but it is the necklace of surrounding islets that best typify the staggering beauty of this island group. Here you will find the extraordinary Frégate Island Private.

Frégate Island is a tiny speck on the edge of the Seychelles archipelago. This 740-acre jewel is home to a beautifully integrated boutique hotel, Frégate Island Private, where man lives in total harmony with nature. Turtles lay their eggs on its sublime beaches, the endangered magpie robin will join you for breakfast at your villa and you can even adopt one of the giant aldabra tortoises that are raised and released into the wild on the island.

frégate island

HOTEL frégate island private

Frégate's sixteen Balinese-inspired villas are perched on granite rocks above the whitest sand imaginable. Each comes with its own walled garden and, as the hotel's name suggests, is totally private. The line between indoors and outdoors is blurred: with full-length windows and a terrace on one side and the ocean on the other, it's like being on a boat with a large deck. You're free to enjoy the silent air-conditioning, but nothing compares to cooling off in the gentle tropical breeze and falling asleep to the sound of the waves below.

Although there is no direct beach access, you can walk or take your own private golf buggy to one of the island's seven *anse* (the Creole word for beach). The hotel beach is a wide expanse of soft sand that offers a bar, beach umbrellas, lounge chairs and excellent service. If clothes aren't your thing, then head to Anse Maquereau; just flip the sign over to read 'Beach Occupied' and it will be yours for the day. The best beach of all, however, is Anse Victorin. A perfect strip of white powder lined with palm trees and flanked by massive granite boulders, it embodies everything the Seychelles are about.

Meals are served wherever you like: your room, on the beach, at the restaurant or the outdoor Pirates Bar carved into the hillside. The ever-changing menu is delicious, all fruit and vegetables

at a glance

Airport	Mahé
Airlines	Air Seychelles
Transfer time	20 mins by helicopter or light aircraft
Rooms	16 (all air-conditioned)
Staff ratio	7+
Activities	Sailing, eco walks, bicycles, golf on Praslin Island, deep-sea fishing, canoeing, swimming pools, tennis, spa, gym
Services	Internet, telephone, television, CD and DVD player
Other	Mobile phones
Children	All ages
Power type	UK 3-pin square
Currency	Seychelles rupee (all hotel bills must be paid by credit card)
GMT	+4
Telephone	+248 670100
Website	www.fregate.com
Booking	www.diveinstyle.com

being organically grown on the island. Dinner is sometimes served at the old plantation house close to the marina, which offers a welcome change of scene – driving there by buggy gives you a real sense of going out for the evening. Wherever you eat, informality is the order of the day, and there's not a jacket in sight.

If you've had enough of your villa or the beach, there is plenty to do, from climbing the peak of Mount Signal to taking a tour of Frégate's nursery for giant aldabra tortoises. There is also a small marina offering everything from canoes and windsurfers to private charters. If that sounds too energetic, you can escape to the truly amazing Rock Spa, a hilltop oasis set among lily ponds that offers a huge range of therapies, including a treatment based on *coco de mer* or sea coconuts, found only in the Vallée de Mai on nearby Praslin Island. There are few more relaxing ways to end the day than having a reflexology massage on an outdoor daybed while you watch the sun set and the terns wheel overhead for as long as your eyes stay open...

Frégate is a truly extraordinary place. It's the closest you will come to having your own private island, but without the headaches of ownership. Three days is the minimum stay here, but if you can manage it, five days would be even better.

all day dining menu
all day dining menu

PLEASE MIND YOUR HEAD
PORT VICTORIA

Frégate is one of the only resorts in the Seychelles with its own marina – important given the seas that sweep these exposed islands – so your boat is just a stroll away from the immaculate dive center. A small wash-down pool hints at the way diving is done here: on such a personal scale that they will not take more than two guests at a time unless you request otherwise. Not only will you not be crowded on your dive, but you certainly won't meet any other divers.

DIVE CENTER

All boats have a dedicated dry area for towels and cameras. Yours might be anything from a 31ft purpose-built dive vessel, fine for calm seas, to the 41ft-deep, V-hulled *Frégate Bird*, which offers a stable, comfortable platform in rougher conditions. The relaxed but thorough briefings take place on land, and you'll find your gear waiting for you on board, fully prepared and ready for your dive.

The dive center's equipment is replaced every two years and is always in first-class condition. The chances are you will not need a computer as the diving here is fairly shallow and tanks are small at ten litres. Nonetheless, you might want to bring one along if you're thinking of doing one of the few deeper dives.

The members of the dive team are among the most experienced in the Seychelles and have discovered most of the dive sites themselves. While they tend to concentrate on the area nearby, you can also opt for day trips to the beautiful islands of Praslin, La Digue or Mahé.

All in all, this is as painless and as personalized as diving gets. If you want to pick up the basics or are a nervous diver, there is nothing less intimidating than learning one-on-one. Like the hotel, the diving here is strictly 'private'.

at a glance

Boats	31ft+ (dry, covered)
Group size	2
Instructors	2
Languages	English
Courses	All PADI
Children	10+
Other	Food and drinks, gear prep and wash down, private charters

ABOVE
Granite boulders make for dramatic underwater landscapes with endless crevices to explore.

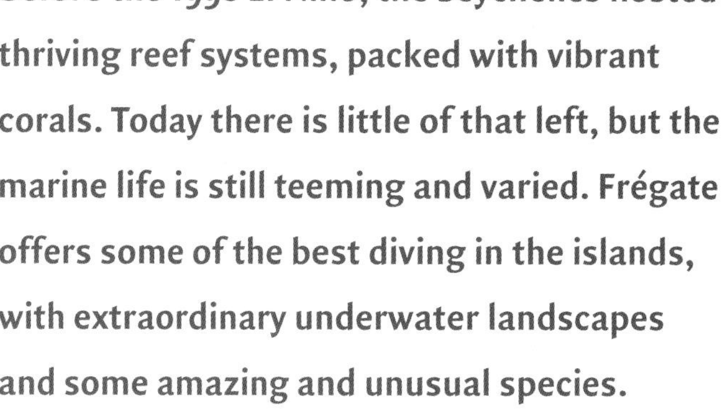

Before the 1998 El Niño, the Seychelles hosted thriving reef systems, packed with vibrant corals. Today there is little of that left, but the marine life is still teeming and varied. Frégate offers some of the best diving in the islands, with extraordinary underwater landscapes and some amazing and unusual species.

ABOVE
A baby emperorfish, even more beautiful when young than as an adult.

RIGHT
A pair of juvenile geometric moray eels.

DIVING

There are about nine sites in Frégate's immediate locale, all under fifteen minutes away. One of the great things about the diving here is that you're almost guaranteed to see what you're after – it's a bit like diving on demand.

The best example of what diving here is all about is Stingray Point. Don't be fooled by the apparent desert beneath you. This is home to the rare Indian Ocean walkman and the extraordinary shovelnose ray: fierce looks, shark fins and a threatening shark shape, but in reality a ray in shark's clothing – worrying to behold but totally docile, feeding on seashells and other sand-dwelling creatures. You can also expect to see the bowmouth ray, a rarer member of the same family, as well as manta ray and smaller life such as anemone crabs.

The seabed is for the most part a gently descending floor of sand, interrupted by the occasional bommie teeming with life: you might see a family of geometric, honeycomb or yellow margin moray on one, catfish and glassfish on another. And while you focus on the small, you could well be interrupted by the noise, literally the noise, of an enormous school of mackerel appearing out of the murk like something from *The Blue Planet*.

at a glance

Local sites	14
Level	Easy to advanced
Visibility	50–100ft
Must-dives	Stingray Point, Lion Rocks
Snorkelling	Good (ask hotel for directions)
Wetsuits	3mm
Coral	Poor
Marine life	Indian Ocean walkman, eagle ray, schools of unicornfish, big eyes and mackerel, manta (November–January), bowmouth, shovelnose, fantail and porcupine ray, green and hawksbill turtle, honeycomb and guineafowl moray, reef sharks and nudibranchs
Other	Hyperbaric chamber at Victoria on Mahé (20 mins), day trips to Mahé, Praslin, La Digue, Marianne and Shark Bank

RIGHT
A school of juvenile striped eel catfish seek safety in numbers.

ABOVE
A pregnant yellow pufferfish, considered a culinary delicacy in Japan, despite its highly toxic flesh.

LEFT
The attractive honeycomb moray, the most docile and approachable of eels.

RIGHT
The weird, wonderful but shy unicornfish, which schools in the waters of the Seychelles.

ABOVE

A manta ray glides by at Stingray Point.

LEFT

Granite blocks from a giant's construction set are awesome to look at and provide shelter to many types of marine life.

ABOVE

A ray in shark's clothing: the extraordinary shovelnose ray.

BELOW

Curious and friendly Atlantic spadefish often accompany you closely on dives.

BELOW
Schools of fish such as jackfish are common around Frégate.

RIGHT
The extraordinary Indian Ocean walkman is rare but seemingly always found at Stingray Point.

MIDDLE RIGHT
Large nurse shark are approachable but known to bite. They are armed not with traditional rows of teeth but powerful grinding plates.

BOTTOM RIGHT
Porcupinefish are an unpalatable meal for predators. Not only do they swell to twice their size, they also exhibit their spines.

Lion Rocks, a field of dead coral that has clearly taken a hammering from El Niño, again offers no shortage of sea life. A more conventional-looking site is Surprise Rocks, whose hard and soft corals are starting to make a comeback. However, the real underwater architecture is created by the huge granite boulders piled on the sea floor – you almost feel like a child poking around a giant set of bricks. Exploring this rocky playpen, you'll find enormous resting nurse shark, soaring devil rays, boxfish, porcupinefish, green moray, lionfish, eagle ray, green and hawksbill turtle, and the usual plethora of tropical fish. Friendly batfish accompany you throughout the dive, occasionally nibbling at your fins while you explore the endless nooks, crannies and overhangs.

Snorkelling can be very good and will appeal to divers and non-divers alike. Provided the seas are calm, the more intrepid can grab a canoe from the marina and pull it along as they snorkel off Airport and Marina Beach. Alternatively, the dive center is happy to advise guests about which beaches are best for snorkelling, as some are more worthwhile than others.

The diving here is very easy and suitable for all levels. The water is not deep, nor is there much in the way of current, so it's an ideal place for learners. An added plus is that on surfacing, you are rewarded with the stunning sight that is Frégate Island, a reminder of the luxuries that await you on your return.

Go now while you still can. These low-lying islands off the west coast of Sri Lanka will be among the first to disappear as sea levels rise due to global warming. The loss will be devastating, not only to the Maldivians but also to the 300,000 annual divers and visitors. These 1,190 unique jewels are strung out like a necklace from north to south, spread over some five hundred miles of the Indian Ocean. Totally unspoilt, they offer a breathtaking sight from the plane before you even touch down.

Development here is strictly controlled, the maxim being 'nothing higher than a palm tree', and marine life enjoys similar protection as there is no real commercial fishing. Only fifteen per cent of the islands are inhabited, with about a quarter of the population living on Male, so there are more than enough islands to go round between locals and visitors. Virtually wherever you go, you feel a million miles from anywhere.

There is a marked difference in diving between the northern and southern atolls, so it is worth trying to do both while you're in the region. Thankfully you won't have to compromise on accommodation: whether you venture to Soneva Fushi in the north, Dhoni Mighili in the south, or stay on a luxury floating Four Seasons somewhere in between, there are few more desirable places to stay. These exceptional destinations, along with the country that hosts them, are exactly what diving in style is about.

Located a third of the way down the southern Ari atoll, Dhoni Mighili is a tiny palm-fringed island with perfect white-powder beaches and the clearest aquamarine waters imaginable. A toes-in-the-sand hideaway, the hotel that sits on it was voted the most romantic in the world by *The Sunday Times* in 2004 – and rightly so. Staying here is a Robinson Crusoe experience, but with an added bonus that Crusoe would have given his right arm for: a boat.

dhoni mighili

HOTEL dhoni mighili

Once you land on Male, it's up to you how you get to Dhoni Mighili. Either you take a short seaplane ride and gaze down at the stunning turquoise inkblots below, or you make your way to the water's edge a few yards from the airport and step aboard your own private dhoni, with its Frette-dressed double bed and a bottle of iced Taittinger to make the four-hour journey more than bearable. Either way, shoes come off the moment you hit the jetty and you cast your cares away.

Dhoni Mighili is all about chic simplicity. A sand-floored thatched structure houses the bar, library, dining room and small boutique. Here you are introduced to your personal *thakuru* or butler, who will assist you with any of the myriad choices available to you during your stay. The atmosphere is appealingly informal: there is no timetable, nor do you have to fill out forms when you check in – you can do this at your leisure any time before you leave.

The hotel has just six elegantly simple rooms, with cool hardwood floors, ceiling fans, air-conditioning, espresso machine and private bar. Unlike sister hotel Huvafen Fushi, televisions are deliberately absent here, but a Bose hi-fi system and fully loaded personal iPods will keep you entertained (you make your music requests via a questionnaire before you arrive). Set on the beach, these individual

at a glance

Airport	Male
Airlines	Qatar Airways, Bel Air, Emirates
Transfer time	20 mins by seaplane
Rooms	6 private dhonis, each with own beach bungalow (both air-conditioned)
Staff ratio	10
Activities	Private dhoni, watersports, island-hopping, fishing, spa
Services	Telephone, customized iPod, DVD/CD player and television on dhoni, complimentary DVD and CD library
Other	Mobile phones
Children	16+
Power type	3-pin square
Currency	Maldivian rufiyaa, US dollar
GMT	+5
Telephone	+960 666 0751
Website	www.dhonimighili.com
Booking	www.diveinstyle.com

thatched bungalows are mostly hidden from the sea, and while more of a view would be welcome, the upside is that they are very private. All have their own small garden complete with outdoor shower, and four are endowed with a waterfall-fed plunge pool – a wonderful touch, especially when the water is always the perfect temperature.

The island is almost perfectly circular, surrounded by a wide collar of fine white sand that disappears into gin-clear, turquoise-blue waters – the swimming couldn't be better. When you need a break from the sun, the loungers outside your room are ideal for relaxing, or you can recline on a swinging daybed or sofa in one of the small open-sided *undholiges* or traditional Maldivian shelters.

A world of options are available to Dhoni Mighili's guests. Dining, for instance, can be anywhere: in the laid-back restaurant, on the beach by the water's edge, or even by your own plunge pool filled with floating candles. If you ever tire of your room, you can always retire to your dhoni and moor out in the bay for the night.

And what a dhoni: the interiors are totally indulgent, featuring a spacious bedroom complete with plasma screen and Bose sound system, Philippe Starck shower room filled with l'Occitane toiletries, living room and fully stocked Smeg fridge in the kitchen (not your province). Things are no different on deck, where you can sit back on the luxuriously plump cushions and watch the tiny islands slide by. There is naturally a full-time crew of three, plus of course your thakuru, all on hand to cater to your every whim, whether it's lunch on a deserted beach or a trip to some distant island on the horizon.

Dhoni Mighili is a unique gem; there is nothing like it anywhere else in the world. It may be only a twenty-minute seaplane ride from the Maldivian capital, but you feel more isolated here than on many of the more distant islands. What's more, having a luxury boat at your disposal adds a dimension of complete freedom to your experience. Given the island's small size, it is becoming increasingly popular to book the entire hotel, and why not? Staying here is truly unforgettable – and this is before you even consider the diving.

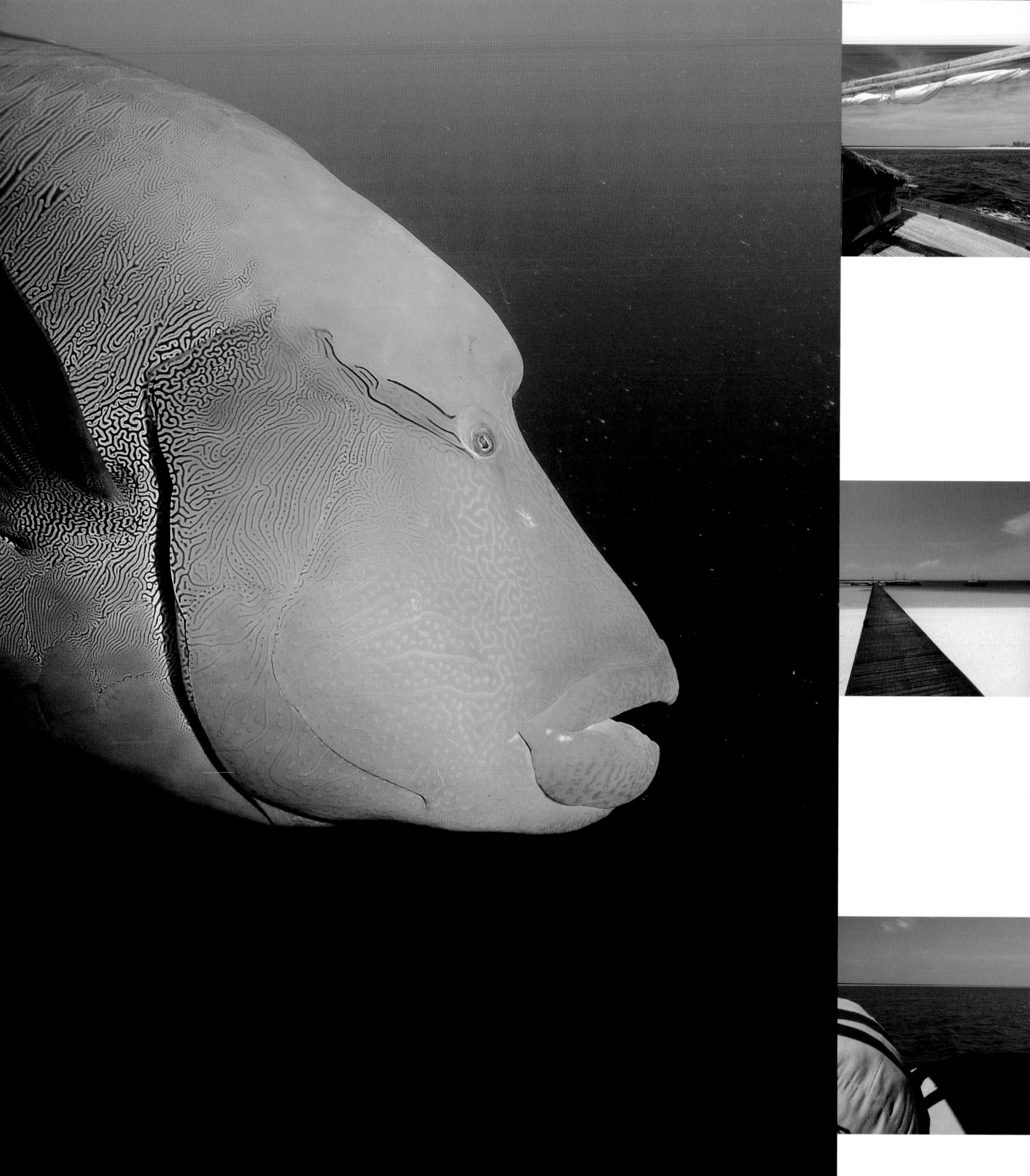

Diving at Dhoni Mighili is as good as it gets, all from the unbelievable comfort of your own dhoni. Everything is tailored to your individual needs, and you never have to think about your gear unless it's on your back. All this would be wonderful in any location, but in the heart of some of the world's very best diving, it is simply magical.

DIVE CENTER

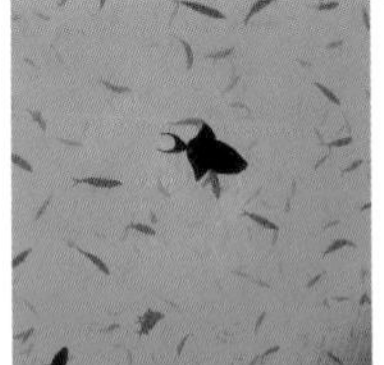

There is no dive center as such, just a permanent instructor who leads groups of no more than two. Meeting up is a casual affair: you head to the hotel bar to fill in the usual forms and plan the days ahead. They are highly conscious of safety here, so if you have any medical issues, the easiest thing is to bring a letter in English from you own doctor stating that he is happy for you to dive.

Everyone has to do a pleasant orientation dive on the 'house reef' (a thirty-minute boat ride). Thereafter, depending on your experience, where you dive is up to you. Like a sommelier, your instructor will guide you expertly through the fine dive list; the southern Ari atoll is truly your oyster, and you can even overnight on your dhoni at more remote sites.

Preparing for a dive could not be easier. Once you select your equipment (dive computers are mandatory), you simply board your dhoni. While you relax on the amazing fat-cushioned daybed, on arrival at a site you will find everything set up on the stern, ready for the dive. If you intend to dive every day, it's best to let them know in advance so any additional staff and equipment can be provided from sister hotel Huvafen Fushi, which has a well-equipped dive center also run by Divers Haven.

at a glance

Boats	Private dhoni (dry, covered)
Group size	2
Instructors	1
Languages	English, French, German, Italian, Japanese
Courses	All PADI
Children	16+
Other	Computer hire, food and drinks, gear prep and wash down
Website	www.divershaven.net

ABOVE
Soldierfish live up to their name. As if on guard, they float motionless in the currents.

The southern Ari atoll hosts some of the bigger sea life in the Maldives, and despite the ravages of El Niño you will find some truly magnificent reef systems. Thanks to the freedom of your own dhoni, the wonders of the diving here are yours to discover, whether you're after whale shark and manta ray or moray and nudibranchs.

ABOVE
Small fish swarm in the water when the coast is clear. The second they perceive a threat, they retreat into the unreachable crannies of coral heads.

DIVING

at a glance

Local sites	6
Level	Easy to advanced
Visibility	50–70ft May to November (wet season), 70–100ft+ December to April (dry season)
Must-dives	Fish Head, Kandholhudhoo, Mayatila, Thundufushi, Madivaru
Snorkelling	Excellent from dhoni
Wetsuits	3mm
Coral	Recovering, soft better than hard
Marine life	Manta and eagle ray, whale shark, hammerhead, white-tip, black-tip and grey reef shark, Napoleon wrasse, moray (4 varieties), pilot whale, frogfish, mantis shrimp, ghost pipefish, large schools of surgeonfish, snapper, trevally, jackfish, barracuda, batfish and unicornfish
Other	Day trips, overnight trips, wreck dives, hyperbaric chamber (10 mins)

Dhoni Mighili is very close to one of the Maldives' most renowned sites, Fish Head, which got its name because at one point local fishermen only ever seemed to bring in fish heads. An inquisitive diver decided to see what was going on and confirmed that underwater was a whirl of life, including the sharks responsible for the fishermen's poor haul. Now this is one of the few protected marine areas in the country, and grey reef shark are virtually guaranteed, along with great schools of fusilier and yellow grunt.

Fish Head is a wonderful dive, but do not expect crystal-clear water as it is in the heart of the atoll. Swept by a constant current, the visibility is probably limited to 50ft or so. However, what it lacks in clarity, it makes up for in action. The site is a rather small oval-shaped reef, and you usually circle it, often accompanied by a large inquisitive Napoleon wrasse. The reef buzzes with activity from all the usual suspects, as well as moray, lionfish, scorpionfish and the occasional passing eagle ray; all this is set against the larger pelagic activity out in the blue.

It's possible to go on a day trip or even overnight in the western fringe of the atoll, where two more world-famous dives await. The first is Thundufushi, a ripping drift dive where the channel

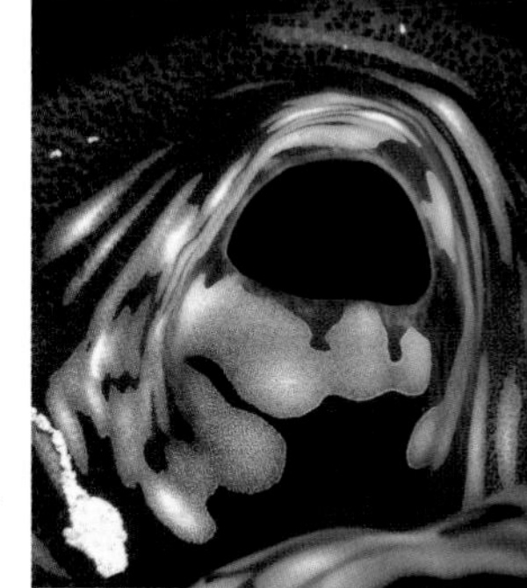

ABOVE
The inside of giant clams come in a seemingly endless variety of stunning colours.

OPPOSITE
Moray eels enjoy a symbiotic relationship with all kinds of shrimp and small fish, which feed off the parasites and scraps that collect around their mouth. It all comes down to trust.

CLOCKWISE FROM TOP LEFT
Surgeonfish are named for the razor sharp scalpels they carry by their tail; year-round encounters with manta are virtually guaranteed in the southern Ari atoll; masked bannerfish are voracious feeders; spotted eagle ray in the Maldives seem less shy of divers than their Caribbean cousins.

RIGHT
Guineafowl moray can be seen hunting away from their lair even during the day.

BELOW RIGHT
The Maldivian reefs are filled with all manner of brightly coloured fish. This blue-faced angelfish is especially vivid.

walls are painted with a suffusion of soft corals populated by schools of bannerfish, butterflyfish, blue surgeonfish and hawksbill turtle. The dive ends in a show of nature's powers of recovery, where large areas of table corals have re-established themselves in a matter of a few years, perhaps testament to the nutrient-rich waters that rush through this pass. In the right tides this can also be a good place to see manta, and it is great for snorkelling when conditions are calm.

The second, Madivaru, is even further south; keep your eyes peeled for whale shark and pods of pilot whales as you cruise outside the reef. Not to be confused with Rasdhoo Madivaru in the northern Ari atoll, famous for its schools of a hundred-plus hammerhead shark, this site is a well-known cleaning station for manta ray. It pays to listen to your instructor and stay low on the reef as you'll be able to witness manta circling above, with wingspans as wide as 15ft.

Manta are just part of Madivaru's appeal. This is clearly Moray Central, and you will see any number of green, honeycomb and guineafowl moray, some swimming in aggressive pursuit of lunch. Schools of surgeonfish, the inevitable scorpionfish, lionfish and other predators are also in large attendance. Don't forget to keep an eye out to the blue, though, as you may well catch sight of the elusive whale shark that cruise these waters year round.

Wherever you venture in the southern Ari atoll, the sea life is prolific, with schools of hunting jackfish, barracuda, fusilier, boxfish, nudibranchs... the list is endless. Best of all, you can enjoy all this from the luxury of your own private dhoni.

Soneva Fushi sits on the edge of the Baa atoll, a thirty-minute seaplane ride northwest of Male. Ringed by perfect fine white sand and waving palms, it is large for a boutique hotel with over sixty rooms, but the beauty of this resort is that somehow it feels more like six. Your seaplane splashes down on a turquoise lagoon, and a three-minute *dhoni* boat ride later, your toes are plunged in pure white sand.

HOTEL soneva fushi

If you have just bought a suitcase full of new Manolos to show off on holiday, this is not the resort for you. The very first thing you are handed on arrival is a 'No News, No Shoes' bag to store your footwear, and from then on, you will have only the sand between your toes.

First impressions of a few low, white-plastered structures set among palm trees give way to the realization that true luxury comes in many forms. The place feels incredibly intimate, designed with meticulous care for the environment, and the natural, almost rugged aesthetic only adds to its charm. Husband and wife team Sonu and Eva (hence Soneva) have a very distinctive touch, which extends to Soneva Gili (pictured opposite, top right and bottom left), the sister resort in the eastern Maldives, which offers truly amazing overwater bungalows. Although the diving cannot quite match that of the Baa atoll, a few days there at the beginning or end of your stay are simply a must, especially as it is just a speedboat ride away from Male.

At Soneva Fushi, each room has its own character, and it is this lack of uniformity that makes the resort so special. Room sizes range from five hundred square feet to nearly five times that, but all benefit from the same comfort, flair and attention to detail: oiled

at a glance

Airport	Male
Airlines	Qatar Airways, Bel Air, Emirates
Transfer time	30 mins by seaplane
Rooms	65 (all air-conditioned)
Staff ratio	4+
Activities	Fishing, watersports, table tennis, badminton, cultural excursions, tennis, volleyball, swimming pools (private), spa, gym (private)
Services	Telephone, television in some rooms, internet in library, DVD and CD player, room service
Other	Mobile phones
Children	All ages
Power type	3-pin square
Currency	Maldivian rufiyaa, US dollar
GMT	+5
Telephone	+960 660 0304
Website	www.sixsenses.com
Booking	www.diveinstyle.com

NO NEWS
NO SHOES

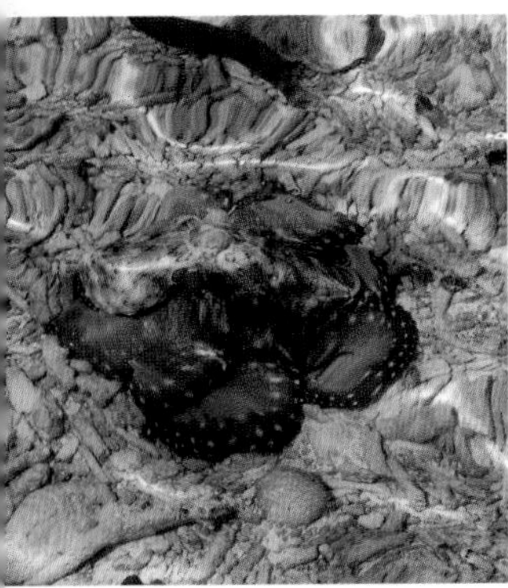

timber floors, white-plastered walls accented by warm burnt-orange fabrics, indoor and outdoor daybeds, bedside lights you can actually read by, a huge choice of pillows, endless fluffy towels and robes, massive bathrooms (some even float on their own lake opening onto a private garden with walls of waterfalls)... And just in case you need anything else, a team of over three hundred staff are on hand to oblige, headed by your personal Man Friday.

The island is criss-crossed by a network of sun-dappled sand paths (naturally brushed clear of leaves every day), which you can choose to travel either on foot or by bicycle. A handful of cosy shops are sprinkled along them, giving the resort the feel of a small village.

Meals are served wherever you like; all you have to do is ask. The menu is astoundingly diverse, catering to all tastes, whether you fancy a hamburger, a spicy curry or anything in between. What's more, everything is faultlessly prepared. And for guests who have a sweet tooth, the island's own ice cream shop – unique among tropical resorts – offers no less than sixty-four different flavours.

Soneva Fushi is a very special place. Its owners continually strive to reach new heights. They dream it then build it, upgrading villas, adding private pools, and incorporating new designs. It is simple luxury, or rather luxuriously simple. Every aspect nudges perfection. Whatever else you do, beat the sea and come here now.

SOLEN
DIVE CENTRE
SONEVA FUSHI

Soleni Dive Center is perfectly run by Thomas and Alessandra, who have been at Soneva Fushi for over a decade. It works like a Swiss clock – appropriately, as Thomas himself is Swiss. This is probably the most experienced dive team in the Maldives, and its members are not so much instructors as underwater bush guides. They have an intimate knowledge of the reefs, and this makes the world of difference to your diving experience.

DIVE CENTER

There are usually two dives per day, at 9.30 a.m and 2.30 p.m. The jetty is no more than 100ft from the resort's main restaurant, so after filling up on breakfast or lunch, you only have a very short stroll to the boat. It's therefore worth taking along your camera, computer or whatever else you need when you leave your room in the morning.

The rest of your dive gear awaits you on board, freshly rinsed and dried by the ever-helpful dive team. A basic basket system is operated: your equipment is kept in a basket on the boat, and you simply put it back after your dive. Once you rig your own BCD, your tank is stored until you reach the dive site.

The purpose-built dive vessel is a modern interpretation of a dhoni, with masses of deck space, a WC and a large sun deck laden with fat cushions. It makes day trips to the more distant reefs very enticing, especially as it cruises almost twice as fast as a traditional dhoni.

There are plenty of instructors with endless language skills, and diving in small groups is their speciality. They seem determined you should see everything and know the sites so well that you will not be disappointed. Interestingly, we dived the same reef with a different team and didn't see half of what Soleni showed us. I rest my case.

at a glance

Boats	35ft luxury dhoni (dry, covered)
Group size	6
Instructors	5
Languages	English, French, German, Italian, Spanish, Japanese
Courses	All PADI
Children	10+
Other	Computer and underwater camera hire, dive shop, nitrox, food and drinks, private charters, gear prep and wash down
Website	www.soleni.com

ABOVE

The Maldives were seriously hit by El Niño, but some areas have escaped. A rare piece of vibrant pink coral juts out from a wall.

If you were lucky enough to dive the Maldives ten years ago, you would have found them utterly spectacular. In 1998 they were devastated by El Niño, which is said to have destroyed ninety-five per cent of the region's coral. Thankfully nature is making an amazing comeback, largely thanks to the nutrient-rich currents that sweep the area. Soft corals are once again plentiful, while hard varieties, including cabbage and staghorn corals, are slowly but surely reappearing.

DIVING

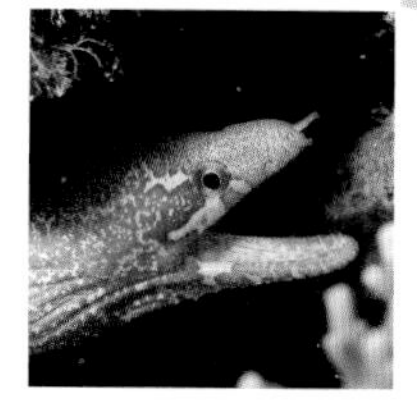

What has not changed is the sheer quantity and diversity of marine life. Diving the Maldives used to be truly magical, a real fairytale, but today it remains fantastic by anyone's standards. Here, on the Baa atoll in the north, you will come across everything from nudibranchs to manta ray, frogfish and stonefish – these islands have it all.

The only species in decline is shark, ruthlessly fished for their fins: every year a shocking hundred million of them are killed worldwide to cater to culinary demands in the Far East. Although the Maldivian government continues to permit this practice, only whale shark numbers seem relatively unaffected. However, there are a few dive sites where shark do enjoy limited protection – here you can still find white-tip, grey reef, silky and, if you are very lucky, scalloped hammerhead shark. But by and large, divers will have to be content with species such as mantis shrimp, stonefish and Napoleon wrasse, whose lips are regrettably another Eastern delicacy.

The Baa atoll provides some of the easier diving in the Maldives thanks to its unusually wide channels, whose currents tend to be less severe than elsewhere; be aware, though, that the year's strongest currents are in January. That said, unless you go on a day trip, most of the dives you will do are on the local *thilas* or

at a glance

Local sites	12
Level	Easy to advanced
Visibility	50–70ft May to November (wet season), 70–100ft+ December to April (dry season)
Must-dives	Nelivaru Thila, Daravandu Thila
Snorkelling	Very good on house reef
Wetsuits	3mm
Coral	Recovering, soft better than hard
Marine life	Manta and eagle ray, whale shark, black-tip and grey reef shark, Napoleon wrasse, moray (4 varieties), pilot whale, frogfish, mantis shrimp, ghost pipefish, large schools of surgeonfish, snapper, trevally, jackfish, barracuda, batfish and unicornfish
Other	Day trips, night dives, marine park, hyperbaric chamber 20 mins

OPPOSITE TOP

The reefs are filled with unusual fish, including this tiny red frogfish.

OPPOSITE MIDDLE

Anemone crabs live within the safety of the stinging tentacles of anemones. They extend their fine fans to sift the ocean for food.

OPPOSITE MAIN PICTURE

The coral may have been badly damaged by El Niño, but this has clearly had little effect on the sea life. Here, on a single coral head, you can see a yellow margin moray, giant green moray, lionfish and marbled shrimp. Believe it or not, just out of the frame there is also a honeycomb moray.

RIGHT

The reclusive mantis shrimp is armed with a powerful club that packs the force of a .22 bullet. It can, and has broken masks, camera lenses and even aquariums.

LEFT
Not all the reefs have been decimated by El Niño. Some are still remarkably untouched.

BELOW LEFT
Schools of grunt are a common sight in the Maldives.

OPPOSITE, CLOCKWISE FROM TOP LEFT
Stonefish are virtually impossible to spot, but the guides at Soleni know exactly where they live; the harlequin ghost pipefish is one of the more delicate and exotic members of the reef community; another species of stonefish, with almost human features; an approachable honeycomb moray.

submerged reefs, more protected from the currents. Although there is a lack of landmarks, Thomas and his crew seem to have no need of GPS, and unfailingly take you to these invisible thilas, which rise to within 15–30ft of the surface. Chances are you won't experience a poor dive; the Soleni dive team know exactly where to go and when.

A favourite destination is Nelivaru, perhaps because it is so close to Soneva Fushi. In season this is a manta cleaning station, but even out of season it has a lot to offer. Fans of moray won't be disappointed: on a single coral bommie, a tiny underwater island surrounded by sand and no more than 20ft around, you might find no fewer than three different species of moray, giving the bommie the look of an underwater Hydra. With help from the Soleni team, you can try and seek out the beautiful harlequin shrimp, a bit like a taunting supermodel who shows you just enough to tempt you, but holds much, too much, in reserve.

Wherever you dive, you will come across an astonishing diversity of life: turtles, frogfish, porcupinefish, spotted, green and black-cheeked moray, hawkfish, lionfish, clownfish, endless anemone, ghost pipefish, scorpionfish, stonefish, pufferfish, schools of snapper and fusilier, boxfish, jackfish, emperorfish, mantis shrimp, stingray... all these and more are regulars to these waters. And in the blue there is a good chance of spotting anything from tuna and trevally to manta and eagle ray.

The tourism figures say it all. Despite the effects of El Niño and the tsunami of December 2004, the Maldives continue to be a magnet to divers and other visitors. These natural setbacks have failed to spoil the beauty of these islands, either above or below the water. You can do no better than allow Soleni to show you the truth of this.

The *Four Seasons Explorer* is hardly recognizable as a live-aboard. It is in fact a floating Four Seasons resort, with all that implies. Launched in 2002, this 128ft catamaran has been skimming the turquoise seas of the Maldives to rave reviews. Cruises start and finish at the Four Seasons Kuda Huraa, voyaging to the northern and southern atolls on alternate weeks. One thing is certain: you certainly don't have to be a diver to enjoy this seafaring adventure.

four seasons explorer

BOAT four seasons explorer

The *Explorer* is arranged on just three levels and offers plenty of covered and open deck space. You'll find everything from a fully equipped dive zone to an extensive library, external bar, jacuzzi, spa, dedicated sun deck and dining room with plasma screen for video presentations of your adventures and basic marine biology talks.

The boat sleeps a maximum of twenty-two guests in the light, elegantly simple staterooms. Their main features are the luxurious signature Four Seasons beds and the wide panoramic windows, which give wonderful views as you journey through the islands. No detail has been overlooked, be it soft linens and towels, excellent storage space, or your own CD/DVD player and television. Two lucky passengers can sleep in the ultimate bed on board in the form of the forward stateroom. This spans the full width of the ship and enjoys amazing panoramic views as well as its own private terrace.

Activities might include island tours, lunch on a remote sandbar or an evening barbecue on a deserted beach (the food is delicious), but you will still have time to swim, enjoy a massage or generally chill out. Perhaps the best indication of the *Explorer*'s appeal is that only fifty per cent of guests are divers. There is no live-aboard like it anywhere in the world.

at a glance

Airport	Male
Airlines	Qatar Airways, Bel Air, Emirates
Transfer time	15 mins speedboat (3 & 7 night cruises), 30 mins seaplane (4 night cruise)
Rooms	10 plus 1 suite (all air-conditioned)
Staff ratio	2+
Activities	Village trips, watersports, island picnics, fishing, spa treatments, marine biologist
Services	Telephone, television, internet, DVD and CD player
Other	Mobile phones (sporadic)
Children	10+
Power type	3-pin square
Currency	Maldivian rufiyaa, US dollar
GMT	+5
Telephone	+960 6644 888
Website	www.fourseasons.com/maldives
Booking	www.diveinstyle.com

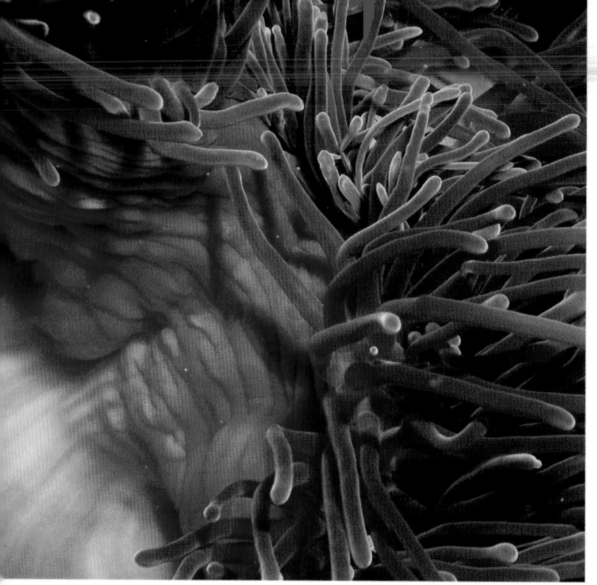

ABOVE
The vivid colours of the underside of an anemone.

Just when you think things can't get any better than on board the *Four Seasons Explorer*, it's time to get into the water. Your diving experience will depend on the itinerary you select, so if you have already stayed in the north it is worth choosing a cruise in the southern atolls and vice versa. Wherever you go, you will experience the best of the Maldives, with the added bonus of diving a greater variety of reefs than you could staying at any one location.

DIVING

The *Explorer*'s spacious dive deck opens to the stern, where your neatly folded wetsuit awaits you. You can choose from an excellent range of dive gear, including flashlights and computers, and it's up to you whether you dive with nitrox or straight air. The dive sites can be anything up to twenty minutes away from where the Explorer anchors. This is no hardship, however, as you dive from a 30ft dhoni, perfectly laid out as a dedicated dive boat. This gives you both shade and cover in case of poor weather and you can even have your tank refilled without returning to the mother ship.

Most dives are done in small groups, but sometimes they will verge on the larger side. Thus if size matters to you it's best to request a smaller group specifically; for a small premium, it is even possible to arrange for your own dedicated instructor. Normally there is a morning and afternoon dive, plus the occasional dawn or night dive.

Dives range from easy sites suitable for snorkelling to fairly serious drift dives. You can also explore some of the Maldives' main channels to the open ocean, increasing your chances of seeing manta and other pelagic life. Best of all, you get to dive an amazing diversity of sites. Going to bed in the luxury of a Four Seasons and then waking up in reach of brand new dive sites – this is a very special experience.

at a glance

Level	Easy to advanced
Visibility	50–70ft May to November (wet season), 70–100ft+ December to April (dry season)
Snorkelling	Good
Wetsuits	3mm
Coral	Recovering
Marine life	Manta and eagle ray, whale shark, hammerhead, white-tip, black-tip and grey reef shark, Napoleon wrasse, moray (4 varieties), pilot whale, frogfish, mantis shrimp, ghost pipefish, large schools of surgeonfish, snapper, trevally, jackfish, barracuda, batfish and unicornfish
Other	Night dives, wreck dives, marine park in some areas, hyperbaric chamber

OPPOSITE, CLOCKWISE FROM TOP LEFT
Scorpionfish, like stonefish, are masters of camouflage and some can even adapt to their colour to suit their surroundings; the famous and almost iconic Shipyard wreck dive is great for exploring; the banded pipefish, small but perfectly formed; looking like a cross between a hamburger and something out of the *Muppet Show*, bivalves are a member of the clam family and while normally found moulded into the coral, do also have the ability to swim.

thailand

The island of Phuket lies just off the west coast of Thailand, a little over an hour from Bangkok by plane. In fact, it barely qualifies as an island – only a narrow channel of water separates it from the mainland – but it is ideally placed to deliver great diving. To the west it is washed by the warm waters of the Andaman Sea, and to the east is the protected Gulf of Phuket, home to the hauntingly beautiful Phang Nga Bay.

Best known for its beautiful beaches and some questionable sex ethics, Phuket will now always be remembered for the tsunami of Boxing Day 2004. Islands such as Koh Phi Phi were devastated, but in Phuket you have to stray from the usual tourist destinations to witness any of the damage. The bulk of the hotels were operating normally within a short time, and they need tourists to return quickly to restore their livelihood. Consequently, Phuket is very much open for business, and you should not be deterred from coming.

Phuket is where you'll find Amanpuri, and your holiday begins the moment you are met at the airport. Any stress from long-haul travel is sloughed off like an old skin while you relax into your Aman ride; a trademark cocoon of white slip-covered seats, lightly scented face towels and chilled Evian all serve as a taste of what's to come. Twenty-five minutes later, already soothed, you enter an almost private headland, home to just two hotels, the Chedi and the incomparable Amanpuri.

Amanpuri was the trailblazer in the now ever-expanding Aman group. It was here, in 1988, that Adrian Zecha first realized his vision of a mouldbreaking style of hotel. Defying the naysayers, he took the concept of luxury to a whole new level, and his ideas now seem like a glimpse of the blindingly obvious. Today, aside from more mature vegetation, Amanpuri looks as if it has just opened, a testament to its timeless design and perfect upkeep.

phuket

HOTEL amanpuri

The centrepiece of the resort is the 100ft infinity pool, now something of a trademark. This Zen-like expanse of midnight-blue water is devoid of clutter and retains its architectural purity. When it was on architect Ed Tuttle's drawing board in the 1980s, it was truly revolutionary, and even today it is captivating. Perfectly reflected in it are the open-sided main buildings: the two restaurants, bar, reception and music pavilion, all overlooked by towering palms, a reminder of the site's former life as a coconut grove.

Forty rooms perch on the hillside, while thirty larger villas with their own pools lie hidden from view. Suspended on stilts, they are accessed by raised walkways and steep stairs, a modern interpretation of a traditional local village, but executed without the slightest hint of Disneyesque parody. It is simply incredibly stylish. These timber-clad structures are ideal for escaping the heat, the sound of birdsong undimmed by their silent air-conditioning. Built in Thai style with soaring roofs, they typify simple luxury. A spacious bedroom with an enormous double bed opens onto an equally expansive bathroom, while a terrace offers a shady chill zone or *sala*. The view varies, and as you would expect, the more of the ocean you want to see, the higher the premium: rooms 103 and 105, with a full sea view, will set you back twice as much as a garden room.

at a glance

Airport	Phuket via Bangkok, Singapore or Hong Kong
Airlines	British Airways or Thai Airways via Bangkok, Singapore, Hong Kong, Japan, Thai Airways to Phuket
Transfer time	25 mins by car
Rooms	40 suites, 30 villas (all air-conditioned)
Staff ratio	4+
Activities	Golf, rainforest, temple visits, watersports, tennis, gym, spa, swimming pool
Services	Internet, telephone, room service
Other	Mobile phones
Children	All ages
Power type	2-pin flat or round
Currency	Thai baht, US dollar
GMT	+7
Telephone	+66 76324333
Website	www.amanresorts.com
Booking	www.diveinstyle.com

The resort itself is spread across some eighty amphitheatre-like broad steps above the beach. The immaculate white-sand crescent is separated from a neighbouring hotel by massive granite boulders, giving you perfect privacy. The swimming is superb, with soft sand underfoot gently sloping to greater depths. White beaches can get very hot in these latitudes, but to give you an idea of the thought and effort that goes into an Aman, every morning a criss-cross network of cooling water is poured onto the sands. As a result, you won't need to hotfoot it uncomfortably from shade to shade.

Lunch is normally at the casual beachside restaurant a few steps above the sand, with a menu that ranges from hamburgers to delicious local dishes. Evening meals are either at the Italian restaurant overlooking the beach or the main restaurant by the pool, where dining is the very essence of tranquillity. The reflective blue-black waters mirror the tall palms and starlit sky, and you are softly lulled by traditional Thai harmonies drifting across from the music pavilion. Meanwhile, your taste buds are aroused by anything from traditional Thai cuisine to outstanding Wagyu beef, all perfectly prepared with spice levels tailored to your preferences. Amanpuri means 'place of peace' in Sanskrit, and this is nowhere more evident than at dinner.

Aman sees Amanpuri not only as their original resort, but as their flagship. While it does host the group's first dedicated spa, overseen by some of the best staff in the business, in fact there is little else to set it apart – every Aman is superb. Like all the resorts by this groundbreaking group, Amanpuri provides discreet luxury in incredibly uncrowded surroundings that subtly echo the individual country and environment. What's more, there is a staff-to-guest ratio that would give any hotel bean-counter a nosebleed. Each Aman is unique, reflecting the local culture and pampering you like nowhere else on earth. But Amanpuri will always be where it all began.

NO DIVING

Unless you are learning to dive at Amanpuri, you will never know there is even a dive center. Once you have booked your dives, whether to the local reefs or the Similan Islands, all you have to do is let the reception know your size, and a selection of gear will meet you at the boat. It is utterly painless. The dive operation is run by the efficient H2O Sportz, and Amanpuri ranks at the top of their client list of five-star resorts. This means you do too.

DIVE CENTER

H2O Sportz has a vast array of vessels to choose from, depending on where you want to go and how large your group is – though there are never more than six people to a dive. A small, shady speedboat will get you to the nearer reefs, while a larger, faster boat will be called into service for day trips and overnighting.

Your departure point will depend on the weather; it can either be off the hotel beach, or from one of two harbours, a short drive away. It's easy to arrange a private charter, whether for a distant day trip or a brief outing, and drinks are always provided, with a full lunch for day trips.

A more adventurous choice is to charter one of the Aman fleet to overnight either north in the Similans or east in the Gulf of Phuket. A literal armada of boats is at your disposal, from the 23ft *Sea Ray* all the way up to a 110ft luxury fantail yacht. There is also a 40ft junk, as well as what may be the most exotic of them all, the 90ft *Maha Bhetra*.

Whether it is for one or two nights or more, chartering a boat enables you to dive more remote destinations and, best of all, to get there before anyone else. There is no better means to do this than on the *Maha Bhetra*, surely the most stylish way to dive these waters.

at a glance

Boats	20ft+ (dry, covered)
Group size	6
Instructors	3
Languages	English, German, Russian; French, Japanese or Mandarin on request
Courses	All PADI
Children	12+
Other	Computer and underwater camera hire, nitrox and rebreathers on request, food and drinks, wash down, private charters
Website	www.diveh2osportz.com

The *Maha Bhetra* is a 90ft purpose-built Thai cruiser, constructed to the exacting standards of Ed Tuttle, Aman's extraordinarily gifted architect. Each Aman resort is designed to capture the spirit of its country, and this luxury vessel is no different. There is nothing quite like her, and yet she is clearly Thai. You drift along at a stately eight knots, stretched out on an enormous daybed while some of the world's most dramatic island scenery slips by.

maha bhetra

BOAT maha bhetra

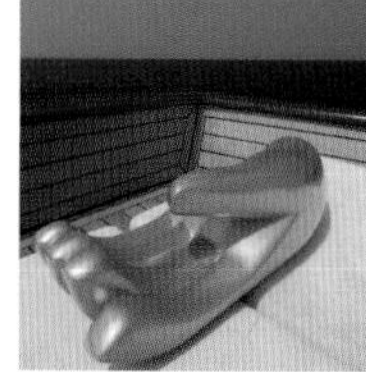

Remarkably, this boat was featured in the very much land-based *Architectural Digest*, and you can see why. There are no visible concessions to adverse conditions. Never bound for Atlantic crossings or storm-tossed waters, her form is perfectly suited to gentle cruises over calm seas in a climate where there is a constant cooling wind. She would be unsaleable and virtually unusable in the Mediterranean or the Caribbean, but she is ideal for the Andaman Sea and the Gulf of Phuket. Here she has no equal – unsurprising, given such a bold and uncompromising design.

Passengers dwell on two decks: the lofty upper deck, where you will spend most of your time on board, and the lower deck, which gives access to the cabins. There are just three air-conditioned double bedrooms, all beautifully finished in local hardwood and featuring a vast bed, generous shower area, vanity unit and masses of cupboard space. They open to the deck on both sides, with the master suite opening out on three sides. There are no corridors on this boat; you are always within view of the sea.

The upper deck is a covered, open-sided living space, offering a huge daybed, dining table and plenty of room for sunbathing. It is also home to the wheelhouse reminiscent of Jules Verne's 20,000

at a glance

Airport	Phuket via Bangkok, Singapore or Hong Kong
Airlines	British Airways or Thai Airways to Bangkok, Thai Airways to Phuket
Transfer time	25 mins by car
Cabins	3 (all air-conditioned)
Staff ratio	2
Services	Thai chef, fishing, canoeing, Thai massage therapist on request
Children	All ages
Power type	2-pin flat or round
Currency	Thai baht, US dollar
GMT	+7
Telephone	+66 76324333
Website	www.amanresorts.com
Booking	www.diveinstyle.com

Leagues Under the Sea, complete with traditional brass wheel, angled glass and massive GPS screen.

As the sun drops lower in the sky, blinds can be let down for shade. The temperature is always perfect, a balmy wind constantly blowing from the east or west depending on the season – you'll never want for air-conditioning. Perched high above the sea, the experience is a bit like the seafaring equivalent of riding in a 4 x 4, looking at the world around you from your comfortably lofty vantage point.

You can take out the *Maha Bhetra* for up to seven days; it's up to you whether you venture north to the Similans, or southeast to Koh Phi Phi. Both routes offer amazing diving, but while the scenery in Phi Phi is dramatic, probably your best bet for diving is the Similans. The biggest advantage of even a one-day cruise is the chance to visit the dive sites before anyone else – you dive on your own. While there is no dedicated dive area on board, divers are very well catered for; if you don't dive or want a break from the water, then the daybed is an appealing alternative.

The best thing about the *Maha Bhetra* is that you are never separated from the beauty of the Thai islands; there is not so much as a sheet of glass to come between you and the surrounding scenery. The design is literally inside–outside, and you are protected from the sun and cooled by the winds, all the while being waited on hand and foot. This is surely the most sybaritic, stylish luxury you will find afloat.

ABOVE
Under threat, poisonous pufferfish inflate to several times their size to look like an unmanageable mouthful to predators.

Diving in Phuket is incredibly diverse, and Amanpuri caters to it all. While you can dive locally, you will be rewarded by venturing further on one of the hotel's fast boats to the Similan Islands, the finest diving Thailand has to offer. Here you will encounter stunning scenery, clear waters and 100ft visibility; stay local and the visibility will be about half that.

DIVING

Day trips can be done either by private charter or in small groups. It takes about two hours to get to the Similans, normally only accessible between November and April due to weather conditions. The crossing may be challenging, but once you get there the lee of the islands offers extensive protection. Even if you are not a diver it's worth coming along – you might see leopard shark on the surface, for instance. Provided the weather cooperates, this trip is a must.

The Similans have some world-renowned dive sites with plenty of variety, from gently sloping walls to the east and dramatic boulders such as Elephant Rock to the west. Once subjected to dynamite fishing, the area has been a marine park since 1982, and it is now inhabited by a huge variety of life. There are some pristine reefs, thick with hard and soft corals, inhabited by green turtles, giant green moray, snowflake moray, yellow margin moray, octopus, leopard shark, cuttlefish, schools of anthias, pikefish, butterflyfish, lionfish and coral groupers, while jackfish and mackerel hover in the deep awaiting their moment. It's all here, and in the right season, you may even see whale shark and manta ray.

Closer to home are a number of sites, again accessible by day trip. Anemone Reef and Shark Rock are absolute must-dives.

at a glance

Local sites	6 (for hotel)
Level	Easy to advanced
Visibility	50–80ft in bay, 80ft+ on west coast and Koh Phi Phi
Must-dives	Anemone Reef, Shark Rock, Similan Islands
Snorkelling	Good on house reef and *Maha Bhetra*
Wetsuits	3mm
Coral	Excellent
Marine life	Leopard shark, ghost pipefish, seahorse, harlequin shrimp, yellow, snowflake, banded-ring and white-eyed moray, clownfish (5 varieties), whale shark, green and hawksbill turtle, manta ray (at Hin Daeng and Muang), shovelnose ray, schools of sea pike and yellowtail fusilier
Other	Day trips, night dives, wreck dives, 2 hyperbaric chambers in Patong Beach and Deep Sea Port

OPPOSITE TOP LEFT
The ornate harlequin ghost pipefish is one of the most delicate, beautiful and elusive of all marine species.

OPPOSITE TOP RIGHT
Scorpionfish are so well camouflaged that you can only see their colours with artificial light – watch out when looking for a handhold in a current.

OPPOSITE BELOW
Anemones curl into a ball when they sleep, displaying their mouth and vividly coloured underside. Under a flashlight they take on an almost ethereal glow.

OPPOSITE, CLOCKWISE FROM TOP LEFT
Octopus normally hide in their lairs but occasionally come out to investigate; porcupinefish live up to their name when threatened, erecting their spines to put off predators; immaculate green turtles are common in the Similans; stinging jellyfish offer a safe mobile home for a variety of sea life.

RIGHT
Lionfish carry a potent poison in their fan of spines, but are safe to approach closely.

BELOW RIGHT
Snowflake moray, one of the most docile and appealing of the 120 species of moray, are quite common around Phuket, if a little shy.

The visibility may not be perfect, but it hardly matters. The sites are on the eastern side of Phuket, about an hour from the marina, and it is worth getting here as early as possible as it does get busy.

Shark Rock is where you go to find the beautiful leopard shark, which in this protected zone is spared the barbaric practice of finning; if you are lucky you will also find seahorses. Anemone Reef, nearby, is perhaps even more rewarding. The reef itself is relatively small, coming to within 15ft of the surface, but there is such a profusion of life that you simply cannot cover it all in a single dive. It is aptly named: anemones create an all-enveloping cloak, clinging to every surface. Waving back and forth in the surge, they reveal a myriad of life beneath; ghost pipefish, endless varieties of moray, unusually coloured scorpionfish, lionfish, giant map pufferfish, boxfish, nudibranchs, staggering cowries... even if you spend days there, you may not see more than half of it.

An added plus of diving the Gulf of Phuket is the extraordinary surface scenery. It's hard not to find your surroundings jaw-dropping when you surface, and whether you are a diver or not, you should spend a day on the water just to behold the beauty of Koh Phi Phi, the location for the film *The Beach*, and James Bond Island, among others.

The very best way to cover these dive sites is with a private charter, on one of Aman's luxury fleet; this ensures you can dive at dawn and have the site to yourself. Failing that, any of them are still worth a day trip – just make sure to get there early. Surprisingly, even after the terrible tsunami, the reefs are incredibly healthy and filled with a wonderful variety of life. This is truly great diving.

philippines

Consisting of some 7,100 volcanic islands and islets, many of which don't even have a name, the Philippines seems to float on its own in the Pacific. Separated from Indonesia and Indochina by miles of ocean, its history is relatively undramatic; unlike many of its neighbours, it has not seen the rise and fall of dynasties. This may be due to the archipelago's linguistic, cultural and racial diversity – over 111 dialects are spoken in its various regions.

The Philippines has the distinction of being the only Catholic nation in Asia. This is thanks to the strong Spanish influence, which began when Ferdinand Magellan first set anchor here in 1521. While Muslim separatists on the island of Mindanao are a source of some much-publicized unrest, the great bulk of the country is peaceful. You're highly unlikely to notice these rumblings if you stay at Amanpulo.

Located on the private island of Pamalican in the middle of the Sulu Sea, Amanpulo is just an hour's flight south from Manila, but it feels a world away. Your stay in the capital may be no more than a brief interlude in the immaculate Aman airport lounge, but if your flights mean you need to spend a night there, then the Peninsula is the place to go. It's worth arranging for a car to meet you at the airport for the slow crawl into town, but do not be tempted to spend any more time than you have to in this urban sprawl – true luxury awaits you on Pamalican.

Amanpulo *is* Pamalican. The name means 'peaceful island', and it's easy to see why. Pamalican's 250 pristine acres are totally tranquil, with nothing but a luxurious forty-room hideaway, verdant vegetation, exotic bird life and what must be one of the planet's all-time greatest beaches, a seemingly endless stretch of the finest white powder sloping into clear turquoise waters.

pamalican

HOTEL amanpulo

Designed by a leading Filipino architect, the spacious *casitas* or rooms are inspired by the *bahay kubo*, a traditional thatched structure. The twenty-nine beach casitas are incredibly private, discreetly hidden away behind the beach, while the eleven hilltop casitas are tucked further back, some with views towards the neighbouring island of Manamoc – rooms 39 and 40 offer stunning panoramas. In true Aman style, they all feature a huge double bed, two daybeds, a desk area and two walls of windows opening onto your own private deck with yet more daybeds. Rough pebble-washed walls, coconut-shell tables, timber floors and wicker blinds complete the interiors.

There are two hubs of activity: the beach bar and the main building. The beach bar is wonderfully casual, serving drinks and an excellent lunch menu with daily specials. Once a week it transforms itself into a magical setting for a barbecue, where you sit either at a traditional table or on a sumptuous low mattress in Arab style, watching the sun sink behind the blazing bonfire. This is not to be missed.

The main building comes into its own later in the day. Perched on higher ground, this single-storey expanse houses the library, bar and dining room, as well as an extensive boutique. There is also a truly

at a glance

Airport	Pamalican via Manila
Airlines	Air France, Cathay Pacific, Emirates, Philippine Airlines, Qantas, Singapore Airlines
Transfer time	1 hour by plane
Rooms	40 plus 2 villas (all air-conditioned)
Staff ratio	6
Activities	Watersports, tennis, small spa, swimming pool, fishing, sailing
Services	Telephone, television, room service, internet in club room
Other	Mobile phones
Children	All ages
Power type	2-pin flat
Currency	Filipino peso, US dollar
GMT	+8
Telephone	+632 759 4040
Website	www.amanresorts.com
Booking	www.diveinstyle.com

enormous infinity pool, set about with well spaced-out umbrellas and private *salas* – like all Amans, Amanpulo dedicates so much space to each individual guest that you feel as if you're on your own. The secluded, open-sided salas are ideal for relaxing during the day (they all shelter a large, inviting daybed), but they are even better at night – the orchid-strewn pool sala being a simply amazing venue for a private supper. Wherever you dine, the service is always faultless, and the delicious food ranges from traditional Filipino to classic Western dishes.

As you would expect from its incredible stretch of sand, Amanpulo gives you the ultimate beach holiday. There are all the watersports you would imagine, as well as private boat trips to neighbouring islands, and moonlight or sunset cruises. If you prefer to stay on land, you can explore the island from your own golf cart that meets you at the airstrip on arrival, and makes getting around utterly effortless. Just be sure to keep insect repellent to hand and the *nik niks* or sand fleas won't bother you.

Children are brilliantly looked after by carers, but not to worry if you don't have kids – the resort is so spread out that they are never intrusive. Meanwhile, in the background a delightful team of some 250 staff makes sure you never lack for a thing.

All in all, this is the unspoilt Philippines at its very best, in such complete contrast to Manila that it's hard to believe you are only an hour away. Whatever preconceptions you may have of this country, Pamalican, and specifically Amanpulo, totally rewrite them. The hotel is still something of a best-kept secret, especially to Westerners, but it deserves to be a destination resort.

The Dive Shop
PADI

The simple dive center makes for a charming contrast to the perfection of Amanpulo. Housed in a wooden structure at the northern end of the main beach, it is a five-minute buggy ride from virtually any of the casitas. If you have brought your own gear, they will happily collect it for you, otherwise there is a good selection of Sea Quest and Mares equipment available, including children's sizes.

DIVE CENTER

Dives are at civilized times, scheduled for 9 a.m., 10 a.m., 11 a.m. and 3 p.m. Groups can include up to four guests, but usually you will find it is just you and your instructor. The dive team are from Manila but have a good knowledge of the local reefs; they always sport a smile and seem endlessly enthusiastic about the diving here, regardless of how often they go underwater.

You board your boat from the only part of the beach with less than perfect sand, so a pair of wet shoes might be a good idea. The boats provide shade, though expect to get wet on board – not a problem, as you arrive at the dive sites in a matter of minutes. Nonetheless, it is worth taking a waterproof bag if you want to keep your things dry.

Snorkelling is well catered for, with regular trips out to the reefs where you are guaranteed to see masses of fish thanks to regular feeding. The more adventurous can make their own way by taking out a kayak and tying up to one of the designated buoys.

The service here is flawless. You suit up in the shade of the dive center and your gear awaits you on board, where you leave it after the dive. The wash-down service is exemplary; everything is professionally rinsed. It's a great place to learn to dive.

at a glance

Boats	22ft+ (wet, covered)
Group size	4
Instructors	2
Languages	English, Tagalog
Courses	All PADI
Children	8+ (Bubblemaker)
Other	Computer hire, drinks, wash down, private charters

ABOVE

Unlike many of the Philippines' reefs, Pamalican is a protected marine park and undamaged by dynamite fishing.

Pamalican is a self-declared marine park, a rarity in a country notorious for using dynamite and cyanide to catch fish on its reefs. There are two coasts to dive, the more sheltered western shore, where Amanpulo's main beach is situated, and the more open eastern one. Whenever you visit, there is always at least one shore available for diving.

DIVING

All the dive sites are a maximum of fifteen minutes from the center. Few permit mooring, but you will always find the boatman waiting for you when you surface, regardless of weather conditions. Visibility varies, ranging from as little as 30ft on the protected house reef up to 85ft or more at Casita 40, where the open sea seems to clear things up.

Turtles nest on Pamalican and you are virtually guaranteed to see them whenever you dive these waters. The turtles are accustomed to human interaction: Amanpulo looks after their eggs and makes sure that the hatchlings are returned to the wild, and at the right time of year you can witness all of this. Even the house reef, an easy dive just off the main beach, boasts a number of giant green and hawksbill turtles – you might see one gliding by, as big as 6ft from tip to toe, with its shell providing a comfortable ride to a pair of 3ft-long remoras. The fish on the house reef are plentiful too, including blue-spotted ray and yellow margin moray, along with barramundi cod and their beautiful dancing juveniles.

Fan Coral is a dive of a different league. Its immaculate reefs provide home to a panoply of tropical life: lobster, clownfish, emperorfish, Moorish idol, Napoleon wrasse, endless blue-spotted ray and even

OPPOSITE, CLOCKWISE FROM TOP LEFT

A closer look at a giant clam is always rewarding; cobia, like shark, have no swim bladder for buoyancy, so they are forced to rest on the sandy sea floor; clams are incredibly sensitive to movement and will close or withdraw their beautiful mantle when approached too fast; like scorpionfish and stonefish, frogfish rely on camouflage for protection and are almost impossible to see, even when pointed out.

at a glance

Local sites	8
Level	Easy
Visibility	30–80ft+
Must-dives	Casita 40, Fan Coral and The Tip
Snorkelling	Very good on house reef
Wetsuits	3mm
Coral	Very good
Marine life	Cobia, devil, eagle and shovelnose ray, manta ray (December), large green and hawksbill turtles, reef shark, large frogfish, stingray, tuna, flying gunard, blue ribbon eel, nudibranchs
Other	Night dives, marine park, hyperbaric chamber in Manila (2 hrs)

LEFT
Juvenile barramundi are just one of the more unusual and beautiful inhabitants of the reef.

MIDDLE LEFT
The extraordinary flying gunard takes its name from its habit of 'flying' over the sea floor with its wings extended. It is best seen on a night dive.

BOTTOM LEFT
A banded pipefish with its distinctive tail.

OPPOSITE, MAIN PICTURE
Hermit crabs are born without a shell. Like a set of clothes, shells are discarded when they no longer fit and the crab moves up to the next size.

OPPOSITE, LEFT, TOP TO BOTTOM
Clams have a symbiotic relationship with algae, which also adds to their colour; cuttlefish are the traditional source of sepia ink, discharged when they flee; boxfish may be shy, but their striking colouration never fails to attract divers' attention.

the odd giant stingray. This is one of the most appealing dives on the entire island.

Casita 40, located opposite Amanpulo's casita of the same number, is arguably Pamalican's top dive and it is worth diving here more than once. A drop-off from 30ft down to 130ft, this is a thriving reef where you will see enormous inquisitive cuttlefish, turtles and local shovelnose ray. Soft corals seem to be everywhere, while massive sea fans and table corals are making a particularly strong comeback after the devastation caused by El Niño and a major typhoon.

The Tip is something of a surprise dive, filled with unexpected pleasures. Here you can swim with devil ray within arm's reach. Manta and eagle ray may pass by, as well as white-tip and black-tip reef shark, tuna, the inevitable gargantuan turtle, and even 5ft-long cobia. Another great site is the Windmill, located at the northeastern end of Pamalican, facing Concepcion Island. While this drops down to 120ft, divers don't need to venture deep to enjoy its natural beauty.

While the Philippines' very best diving is further south at the amazing Tubbataha Reefs marine park, this is only accessible by live-aboard. Nonetheless, Pamalican comes close. Add in the unimaginably perfect beach, a wonderful hotel, superb service and total privacy, and you soon realize that this is as good as it gets.

palau

Unless you are a seasoned diver or a war buff, it's quite possible that the tiny republic of Palau will not have featured on your radar. Occupied by the Japanese from 1914 until the end of the Second World War, this stunning set of volcanic islands sits out in the Pacific, two hours east of Manila and three hours from Hong Kong. Located midway between the Philippines and Guam in the western part of the Caroline Islands (this eastern part is known as Micronesia), the nation's claims to fame are now its world-class diving and stunning topography.

Palau is not the easiest place to get to. You can fly on Continental Airlines via Manila, on one of two weekly flights, or via Guam, from where flights leave daily; you can also connect from Taiwan. But perhaps it's the country's very remoteness that makes it so special. Its population of just nineteen thousand is spread over some three hundred islands, many of which are uninhabited. As your plane approaches the tiny airport of Koror, Palau's capital, you can gaze down on a pristine paradise of volcanic emerald mushrooms clad in lush vegetation.

Palau's economy relies heavily on tourists, mainly divers, but it is surprisingly difficult to find stylish hotels. The fact is, however, it's impossible to do a grand tour of the world's best diving without coming here. The thing to do, then, is make a beeline for the Palau Pacific on Arakabesang Island, the finest resort in the islands.

If you're looking to stay in a typical five-star hotel, then Palau probably isn't for you. But if you're in search of world-class diving, accessible from comfortable, traditionally appointed accommodation, then you may be in luck. Palau Pacific might not be the swankiest of resorts, but it is by far the best place to stay in Palau. More importantly, it has its very own dive center on site, so diving couldn't be easier.

arakebesang island

HOTEL palau pacific

A gentle thirty-minute taxi drive, arranged in advance by the resort, introduces you to the peaceful nation of Palau. The first thing you notice is there isn't much to see, aside from luxuriant vegetation and a suspension bridge linking the main islands. This really is a backwater of the Pacific, but of course, that's part of its appeal.

Palau Pacific is set in sixty-four acres of lush, tropical gardens, including an amazing orchid farm. Its hub is a high-ceilinged, Fijian-style reception, and various two-storey wings radiate outwards. These are where you'll find the rooms, many of which look out over the sea and the fine stretch of beach.

Where you sleep will make all the difference to your experience. Most of the hotel's 160 rooms are in the older wings, which are somewhat dated – these are best avoided. When you book, make a point of requesting a room in one of the newer wings; you'll be infinitely more comfortable, and you won't even have to pay a premium. Whittling down the selection, your best bet is to stay in blocks 10, 11 or 12, which almost feel like a different hotel. The upper floor offers particularly spacious accommodation, with open, pitched ceilings and small terraces, but you may prefer a room that opens directly onto the gardens. Of course, you can always choose to

at a glance

Airport	Koror via Manila or Guam
Airlines	Continental
Transfer time	30 mins by taxi
Rooms	160, including 8 suites (all air-conditioned)
Staff ratio	1+
Activities	Watersports, hiking, WWII tours, swimming pool, spa, tennis, gym
Services	Telephone, television, room service
Children	All ages
Power type	2-pin flat
Currency	US dollar
GMT	+8
Telephone	+680 4882600
Website	www.palau.panpacific.com
Booking	www.diveinstyle.com

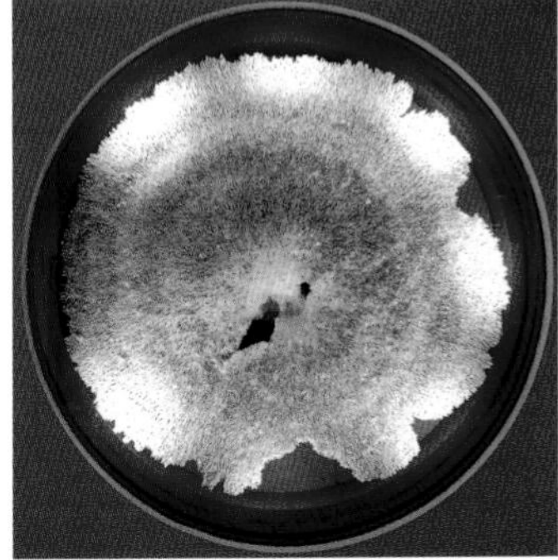

upgrade to one of the eight suites, though again it's safer to stick to the modern sections of the resort.

There are two restaurants, the casual, open-air Coconut Terrace and the slightly more formal, air-conditioned Meduu Ribtal. Their menus have distinct Japanese leanings, with delicious fresh sushi and sashimi served daily. This is easy enough to explain: not only was Palau occupied by Japan for over three decades, but due to its location, many of its visitors today are Japanese.

On most evenings there is a themed buffet at the Coconut Terrace, as well as à la carte options. At the more intimate Meduu Ribtal, cuisine from the Pacific Rim is the order of the day, which is usually centred around local seafood and US beef. You can also choose from an all-day snack menu at the beach bar, or watch the mesmerizing sunset over a private dinner with your toes in the sand.

Speaking of which, Palau Pacific is the only resort in the country with its own private beach, an excellent strip of fine white powder. The house reef is located just off this and offers very good snorkelling; you can even dive here without relying on an instructor. Indeed, the main attraction of Palau is the underwater action. As for the hotel itself, choose the right room and Palau Pacific will give you everything you need for a wonderful holiday. It might not meet the standard of the other hotels in this book, but it is your best option in these beautiful, remote islands.

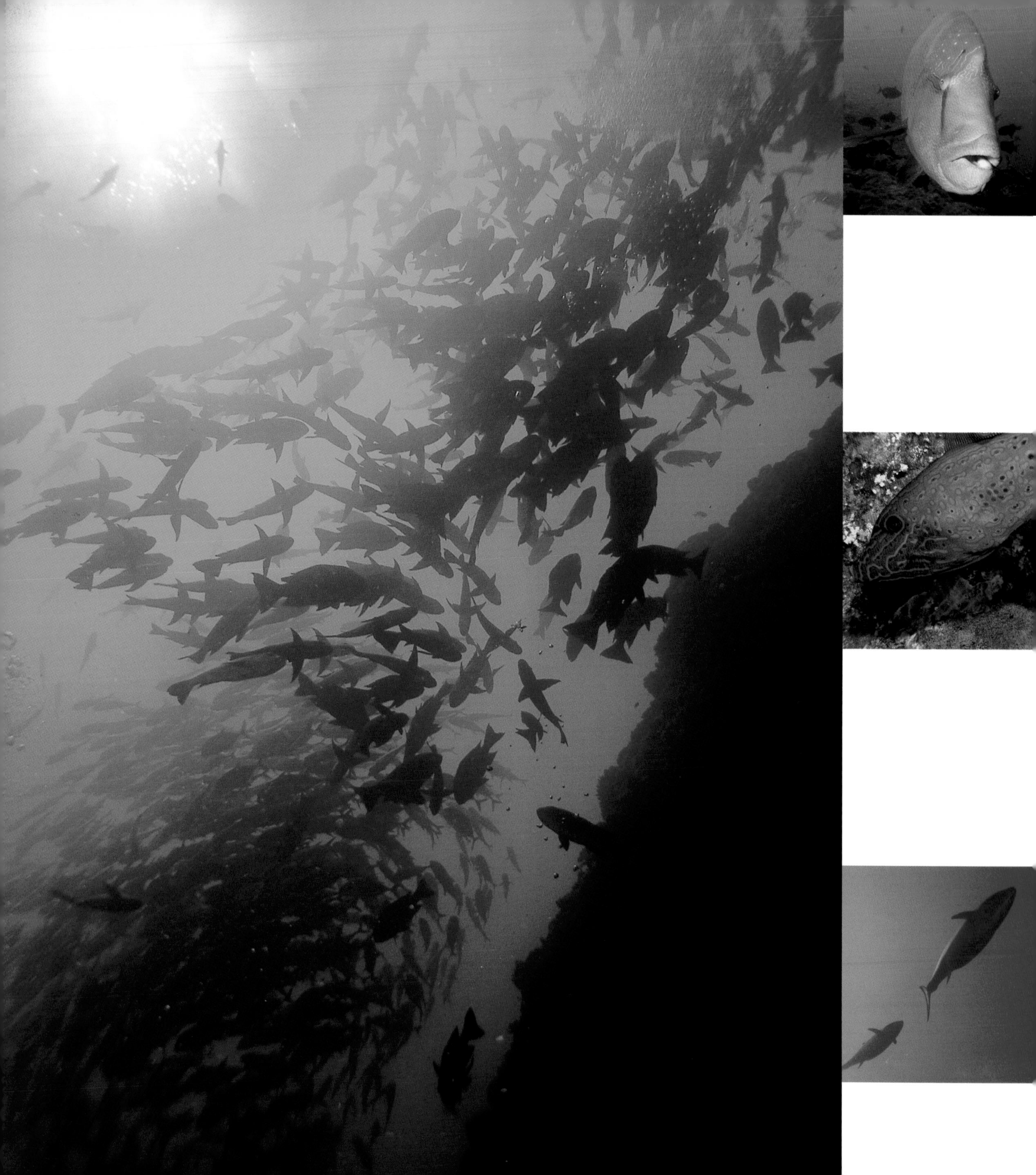

Situated at the end of Palau Pacific's private beach, Splash is a comprehensive dive center with an excellent small shop attached. A short walk away is Photo Palau, which offers film processing as well as a good range of underwater still and video cameras to rent. Alternatively you can dive with Neco Marine, which has an excellent relationship with the hotel; its impressive modern facilities are just a fifteen-minute drive, although they will pick up from the dock.

DIVE CENTER

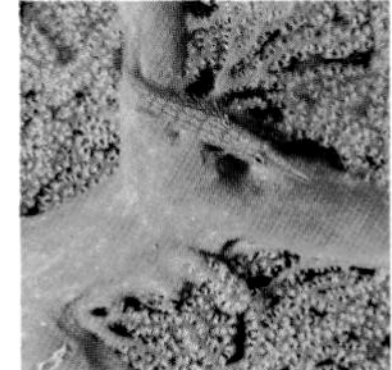

Splash's staff are mainly local but its owners and managers are Japanese, and on day trips you can choose from an excellent selection of Japanese *bento* boxes for lunch. The team are clearly used to dealing with more experienced divers; they don't seem to offer reef hooks, so it's best to be prepared to borrow or buy one from the shop as you will find it invaluable for staying put in the strong currents that sweep some of the sites.

Most dives are done as day trips, and your surface interval after your first dive is normally spent on a sandy beach in the beautiful Rock Islands. The wide-bodied, shallow-draft boats are basic but fine for their purpose.

Your gear is loaded on board in the morning but there is no wash-down service, so it is up to you to take it back to the shop and rinse it. If you'd rather leave this to someone else, help is at hand from neighbouring dive center Neco Marine, which caters to a more Western clientele. They can usually pick up and drop off divers at the resort dock – you just have to arrange this with them in advance. In fact, with their wash-down service, snorkelling trip to Jellyfish Lake (an absolute must), nitrox provisions and wonderful nautilus shell dive, Neco Marine may well be your best bet for diving in Palau.

at a glance

Boats	33ft (wet, covered)
Group size	6
Instructors	6
Languages	English, Japanese
Courses	All PADI
Children	12+
Other	Computer hire, nitrox, food and drinks, private charters, dive shop, underwater cameras to hire, wash down (only at Neco Marine)
Website	www.splash-palau.com www.necomarine.com

Palau offers truly world-class diving, with something for divers and snorkellers at all levels. With over 1,500 species of fish and 700 species of coral, the biodiversity here is truly enormous, and it is all carefully protected by the Koror State Rangers. Blue Corner is Palau's most well-known dive, but there are also plenty of shallow dives, including wrecks suitable for snorkelling.

ABOVE
Action-packed Blue Corner draws divers from all around the world.

DIVING

Blue Corner has entered diving folklore as one of the world's greatest dives; seasoned divers come back year after year, so there must be something to the hype. To get the most out of diving here, try to time it for earlier in the day, when it's usually relatively quiet. You should also probably visit between December and April; it's fine to come in July but the weather might not be so cooperative.

Originally a fishing spot, Blue Corner is washed by powerful currents. Big currents mean big action, so when the site is at its best and most active, you will need a reef hook to keep you in place. While this may sound alarming, there is no need to worry: the plateau you attach yourself to is at just 50ft and you can relax once you are secured with your BC slightly inflated.

The visibility is normally around 100ft but can be up to 150ft, so you should be ideally placed to see the dozens of grey and white-tip reef shark, schools of barracuda, king mackerel, tuna, giant and bluefin trevally, all out in the blue. If you stay close to the plateau, you might also find the odd Napoleon wrasse or spotted eagle ray blocking your view of beyond. On a good day, this is your best chance to see more large pelagics and schools on a single dive than probably anywhere else in the world.

at a glance

Local sites	Many, but best sites 1 hr
Level	Easy to advanced (experience necessary for best dives)
Visibility	80ft+
Must-dives	Blue Corner, Peleliu, Jellyfish Lake, nautilus dive
Snorkelling	Good on house reef, very good from dive boat
Wetsuits	3mm
Coral	Excellent
Marine life	Napoleon wrasse, green and hawksbill turtle, mandarinfish, hammerhead, bull, grey, white-tip and tiger shark, manta, ornate and eagle ray, bumphead parrotfish, large schools of barracuda, jackfish and snapper
Other	Day trips, night dives, wreck dives, marine park

OPPOSITE, MAIN PICTURE
A snorkel at Jellyfish Lake is a magical experience among thousands of jellyfish that have lost their ability to sting.

OPPOSITE LEFT, ABOVE
Randall's goby, one of the smaller and rarer inhabitants of Palau's reefs.

OPPOSITE LEFT, MIDDLE
Nudibranchs, flatworms and wart slugs come in all colours, shapes and sizes in the thriving reefs of Palau.

RIGHT
A nudibranch clearly displays its bare gills; its name literally means 'nude gill'.

OPPOSITE, FROM LEFT TO RIGHT
Whip coral's true colours are revealed by artificial light; yet another variety of nudibranch; while Blue Corner's reefs are almost dead, the rest of Palau's underwater environment hosts thriving hard and soft corals.

BELOW LEFT
A pair of brilliantly coloured mandarinfish: one male, one female. The species is notoriously reclusive.

RIGHT
When the currents are running, Blue Corner can offer a blizzard of large marine life.

BELOW RIGHT
Peleliu was the scene of some of the most violent battles of the Second World War. Today it is peaceful and deserted, and you can explore the dive sites almost on your own.

Palau is far from a one-dive pony, however. You can head to Ngemelis Wall (aka the Big Drop-Off), German Channel for almost year-round manta, or explore one of over sixty wartime wrecks, including a Japanese Zero fighter plane. There are also unique cave dives: Chandelier Cave, in the Rock Islands, is made up of five chambers, the innermost of which is the eerie and aptly named Temple of Doom. Thrill-seekers can venture south to Peleliu, once the scene of some of the most devastating battles of the Second World War. There is a small levy charged for diving here, but this does keep numbers down. There are some six sites, including the Peleliu Express: not for the inexperienced, this is an adrenaline-pumping drift dive that can bring you face to face with anything from large bull or tiger shark to marlin and schools of tuna.

Mandarinfish Lake is home, unsurprisingly, to mandarinfish, which surely must win the prize for the most stunning and perfect of small fish; they are elusive, but visit in the late afternoon as they then tend to rise from the corals at dusk. Another must is Jellyfish Lake. Snorkel to a sunny spot and you will find thousands upon thousands of feeding jellyfish, which have somehow lost their ability to sting. The sensation of swimming with their soft, jelly-like bodies all around you takes a bit of getting used to – you are literally enveloped in them – but this is a truly amazing experience.

And then there's the incredible nautilus dive. Usually deepwater dwellers, nautilus shells are trapped by Neco Marine diving center and then released at recreational diving depths so you can swim with these beautiful, rarely seen creatures. Like so many other dives at Palau, this is simply unforgettable.

indonesia

Indonesia is the world's largest archipelagic state, encompassing some eighteen thousand islands spread over a vast area. A third of these are uninhabited, and many of the rest host little more than a fishing village. In the more remote areas, it's hard to believe that this is the fifteenth most populous nation on the planet, with a population only twenty per cent smaller than that of the USA.

Independent since 1949, Indonesia is an amalgam of many island provinces and has only recently settled into being a democracy. Bali is almost a country within a country, a Hindu island in a predominantly Muslim nation, with one of the most beguiling local cultures in the world. Whether you stay on the coast or up in the hills of Ubud, you are immersed in the traditions of this almost mystical destination: scores of sacred festivals take place each year, when the whole island seems suffused with incense and strewn with flower petals. To top it off, you can stay at some stylish and luxurious hotels. No visit to Indonesia is complete without a trip here.

Travel a bit further, however, and you will find not only wonderful places to stay, but also the greatest underwater biodiversity on earth. Denpasar, Bali's capital, is a major regional hub and easily reached via Singapore and Bangkok. From here you can travel to Moyo Island, home to Amanwana, and on to the stunning waters of Komodo National Park and the timeless *Silolona*.

The remote island of Moyo encompasses some 2,500 acres and hosts a number of small villages, with a total population of only two thousand. On a protected cove in the west lies Amanwana, a secluded hideaway with twenty guest rooms, or rather 'tents'. These aren't just any tents, however. Designed by a Belgian architect to get around a local law dictating that no hotel structure could be permanent, they are a modern and utterly luxurious interpretation of a tent.

moyo

HOTEL amanwana

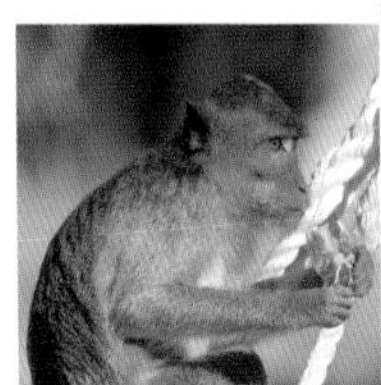

Surrounded by mature tropical forest, Amanwana has no gardens as such, only a sheltered jungle clearing. Nature has been tamed enough to provide a smooth carpet of grass, but that's about it. Invisible birds call to one another endlessly, while playful monkeys scamper around the grounds, occasionally bouncing off your tent roof. You are on both a safari and a beach holiday – a kind of beach safari, with a generous helping of style.

Whatever foresight possessed the Aman group to buy this bay and build a hotel on such a remote island is a mystery, but we should all be grateful that they did. A seaplane will take you direct from Bali and deposit you at the hotel dock, or you can take a direct helicopter charter. From the moment you arrive, the magical Aman ingredients come into play.

If the last time you slept in a tent is an experience you're trying to forget, Amanwana will challenge your preconceptions. An elegant solid structure with a soaring canvas roof, it does a good enough imitation of a tent to satisfy the authorities, but you'd hardly recognize it on a campsite. You can choose between the Oceanfront and Jungle Tents; either is exceptional, but it's worth paying the

at a glance

Airport	Denpasar
Airlines	Garuda, Japan Airlines, Malaysian Airlines, Qantas, Singapore Airlines, Thai Airways
Transfer time	1 hr direct flight
Rooms	20 (all air-conditioned)
Staff ratio	8
Activities	Trekking, kayaking, windsurfing, sailing, deep-sea fishing, small swimming pool, Jungle Cove spa
Services	Telephone, television, DVD lounge, CD player in music pavilion, room service
Other	Mobile phones
Children	All ages
Power type	2-pin round
Currency	Indonesian rupiah, US dollar
GMT	+8
Telephone	+62 371 22233
Website	www.amanresorts.com
Booking	www.diveinstyle.com

small premium for the oceanfront tents' extra privacy and view. Both will give you a huge bed festooned with mosquito netting, a desk, a luxurious open bathroom with twin handbasins and masses of storage space. There are also two L-shaped sofas that are perfect for an afternoon snooze, but also ideal for young children to bunk down on. The typical Aman touches are everywhere: a cotton island map, complimentary sarongs, bowls of exotic fruit, woven sun hats and baskets, all yours for the taking.

There are plenty of dining options. Lunch is informal, served either by the pool or at the open thatched dining pavilion. The simple menu changes daily, with a choice of delicious local and Western starters, main courses and desserts (if you can't take spicy food, you can always ask them to tone down the chilli). In the evening, you can dine at the main pavilion or, for a small premium, keep your toes in the sand by your tent, with your own private bonfire, a table surrounded by hurricane lanterns and a view of the setting sun.

At first glance there doesn't seem to be much to do aside from dive, snorkel or chill, but Amanwana ensures you won't be bored. For instance, the resort offers Hobie Cat cruises, guided jungle hikes and, most memorably, a trip to the island's waterfalls, best early in the year. You take a boat to the local fishing village, switch to African safari mode on an open jeep (take a hat and sunscreen), then walk until you reach the cool clear limestone waterfall pools surrounded by rainforest, where you can take a dip followed by lunch. At the end of the day, you can wind down with a massage at one of Jungle Cove's stone-built treatment rooms, open to the sky and sea.

Amanwana will not give you a beach holiday in the traditional sense. The sand is made up of coarse ground coral, while low tide reveals a craggy seabed. Coming here is about escaping the modern world; being on such an isolated outpost makes you feel like an adventurer, albeit one with more comforts than you can imagine. Most importantly, it's about enjoying the ocean. The water is totally clear and the temperature always perfect, so snorkelling is wonderful (or you can let the fish come to you on the jetty at the 3 p.m. fish feeding). Best of all, while here, you can explore even more of Indonesia on the unparalleled *Silolona* – in effect, a floating Aman.

Amanwana's dive center is located midway between the main restaurant and the dock, where all diving starts and ends. The facilities are fairly simple, but there is an excellent room for teaching and a pair of stylish outdoor showers. However, unless you are learning to dive, you will never need to come here once you have chosen your gear from the good range of Oceanic and Seaquest equipment on offer.

DIVE CENTER

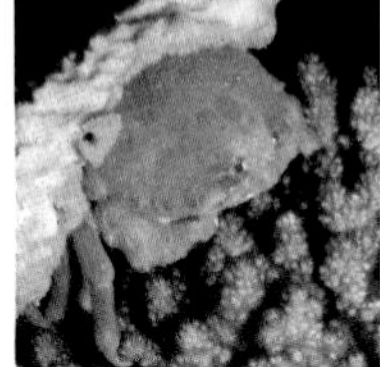

There is something of an armada of Aman boats available, but your main choice will be between a fast 26ft Boston whaler and a much slower 45ft traditional outrigger. The whaler is good for the more distant sites, while the outrigger, with plenty of shade and space for sunbathing, is ideal for a leisurely ride to the local reefs. The rest of the Aman navy means that you'll never be without a boat.

The dive team here is fantastic, and if you are lucky, then Kaz will be there to show you the reefs. He is a true underwater bush guide, able to spot things at a distance that you may find difficult to recognize even close up. Often his underwater horn will go off and you will swim to him, only to follow him even further to somewhere he thinks he has seen something. He always has, whether it's a camouflaged frogfish or a tiny nudibranch. Dive with Kaz and you will never miss out on any of the underwater action.

Even when Amanwana is practically full, you're unlikely to find many other guests diving. In fact, there may be as few as two of you along with one or even two instructors, all to yourselves. How long this place can remain undiscovered by divers is anyone's guess. For the moment, the dive center is something of a best-kept secret, and now is the time to take advantage of it.

at a glance

Boats	26ft+ (dry, open/covered)
Group size	4
Instructors	4
Languages	English,
Courses	All PADI
Children	12+
Other	Computer and underwater camera hire, food and drinks, gear prep and wash down, private charters

ABOVE
The reefs around Moyo explode with a blizzard of marine life.

The sites around Moyo are utterly superb and the coral gives Australia's Great Barrier Reef a run for its money. On top of all this is the most incredible underwater biodiversity anywhere on the planet – it's a true cradle of marine life. You can dive near or far, whether on the amazing local reefs or at more distant sites on day trips. Wherever you go, you'll find wonderfully pristine conditions, and you won't bump into any other divers.

DIVING

Amazingly, one of Moyo's best sites is just a few minutes from Amanwana. Even if you have dived the wonders of the Great Barrier Reef, there is something very special about Panjang Reef. If you have a camera, it's hard to know which way to point it – it's almost overwhelming. The stunning reefs are thriving with dense fields of hard coral – cabbage, staghorn, barrel sponge, sea fan, elephant-ear sponge – and there is no evidence of bleaching.

All this is covered in an undulating wall of marine life. On this dive alone you can see frogfish, nudibranchs, blue ribbon eel, lionfish of all sizes, scorpionfish, leafish, large brown moray and white-tip reef shark, along with a plethora of other species. An added plus of this dive is that although the reef rises from the sea floor some 160ft beneath, its top is only 15ft from the surface, so not a moment of your air is wasted as you explore its many wonders.

Snorkelling is truly excellent, either straight off the beach or from a dive boat on any of the reefs whose peaks almost break the surface. For the adventurous, Amanwana even offers nighttime snorkelling – unheard of at most resorts. Speaking of which, if you have never done a night dive, then this is the place to start. A five-minute boat ride takes you to the old work jetty and the wreck of a timber

at a glance

Local sites	15
Level	Easy to advanced
Visibility	100ft+
Must-dives	Panjang Reef
Snorkelling	Very good on house reef, excellent from dive boat; night snorkelling available
Wetsuits	3mm
Coral	Superb
Marine life	Blue ribbon eel, frogfish, leafish, nudibranchs, manta ray, whale shark, sunfish, white-tip and grey reef shark, schooling trevally, ghost pipefish, pygmy seahorse, bobtail squid, crocodilefish
Other	Night dives, wreck dives, marine park, hyperbaric chamber on Bali (2 hrs)

OPPOSITE MAIN PICTURE
There is so much to see that it's easy to forget the little things. It is always worth checking for smaller life, especially in anemones.

OPPOSITE LEFT, TOP
A night dive at Moyo is particularly worthwhile. All types of unusual life forms come out to feed after dark.

OPPOSITE LEFT, MIDDLE
The tasselled scorpionfish is a master of camouflage and armed with venomous spines, but is only dangerous if stepped on.

RIGHT
A pair of voracious lizardfish wait for dinner to swim by.

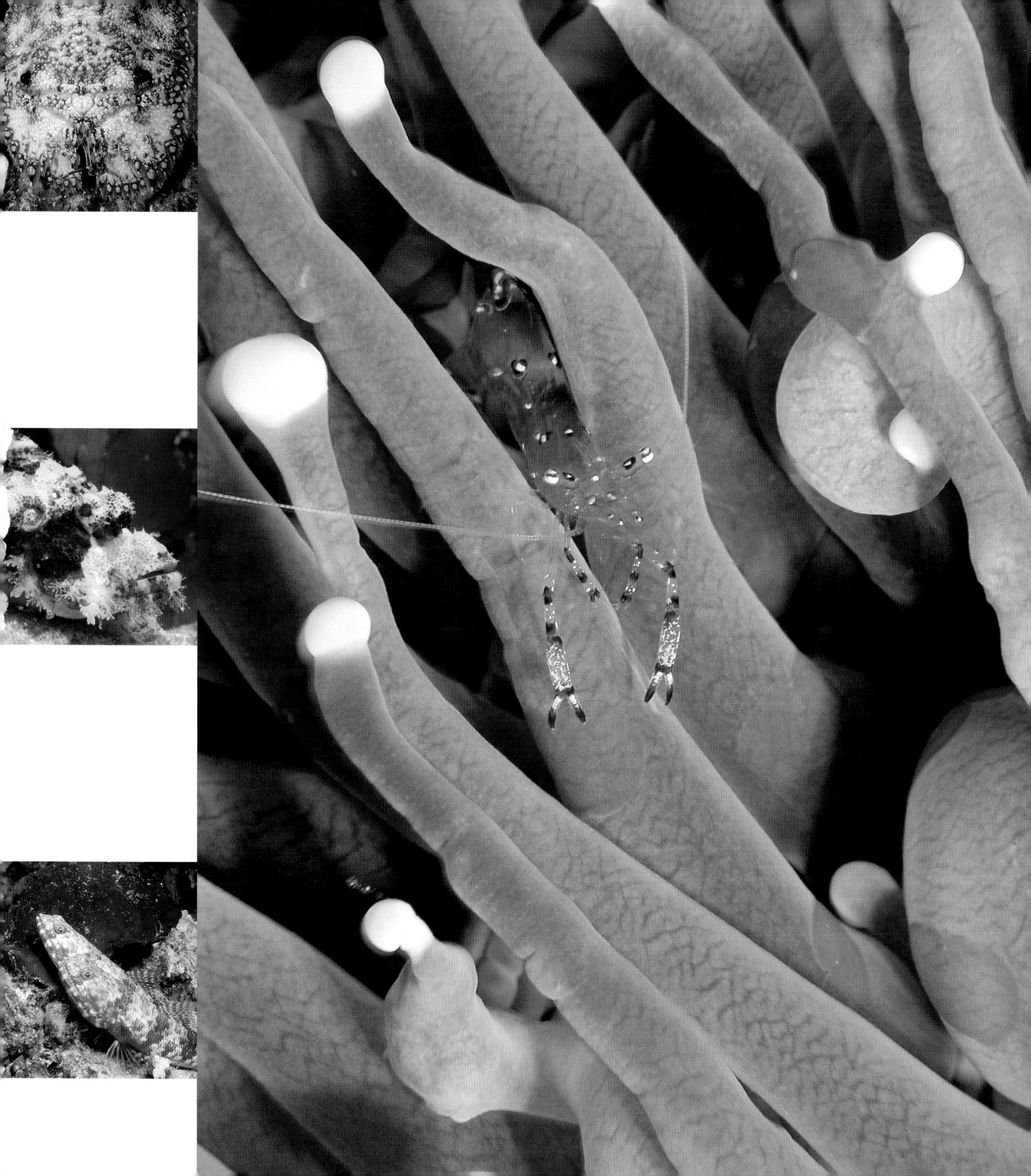

LEFT
Looking like the frills on a shirt, this is actually a nest of nudibranch eggs. The parents are normally close by.

BELOW LEFT
You may not believe that nudibranchs can be the size of dinner plates, but it's true.

CLOCKWISE, FROM TOP LEFT
Vivid nudibranchs are generally found feeding on similarly coloured sponges, thus disguising themselves from predators; the virtually invisible leaf scorpionfish blends into the background by imitating seaweed swaying in the current; the beautiful blueribbon eel changes colour as it changes sex; this may not look like camouflage, but this beautifully patterned frogfish becomes nearly invisible at greater depths.

boat, right off the beach. Here you might come across tiny ghost pipefish, giant sleeping triggerfish wedged in their lairs, parrotfish, scorpionfish, aggressively hunting fimbriated moray or even a clutch of baby moray – all in just a few feet of calm water. Most remarkably, you'll find nudibranchs the size of soup plates. These are something of a revelation: nudibranchs tend to be a few inches at most, but these enormous, almost black varieties (some with a white pattern) are literally twelve inches or more in diameter.

There are a number of other dives around Moyo, all memorable for different reasons: Tanjung Menagis for its amazing garden of soft corals, unicornfish, silver-tip and white-tip reef shark; Angel Reef for giant trevally, Moorish idol and red snapper; and the Wreck, notoriously hard to find, a former fishing boat that is now home to giant scorpionfish, lionfish, crocodilefish, boxfish, nudibranchs, mantis shrimp and ringed pipefish.

It's impossible to see everything during a short stay on Moyo Island. It's so easy to become so entranced by the reef that all the larger life may well be swimming just behind you. Manta ray, green and hawksbill turtle, sunfish, sailfish, whale shark... they are all here, so seeing them is just a matter of luck. Luck aside, you are guaranteed serene diving in wonderfully clear water with no one else in sight, just some amazing sea life. And you get to call the luxury of Amanwana home.

Named after the magical boat of a local legend, the *Silolona* was the brainchild of Patricia Seery, an American steeped in local culture after living in Indonesia for twenty years. With incredible determination, she saw her dream grow into an amazing marriage of traditional shipbuilding skills and the most up-to-date technology. The result is 150ft of floating perfection. There is simply no better way to dive, snorkel or just visit the Komodo archipelago.

silolona

BOAT silolona

The *Silolona* is a *phinisi*, a type of boat built only by the Bugis in the mangrove swamps of Kalimantan, northern Borneo. Over a period of three years, with the help of just one chainsaw, a small electric sander and unbelievable skill, this remarkable craft grew from hardwood trees in the local forest into 150ft of stylish timber boat that now meets the highest German construction standards, more demanding even than those of Lloyd's Register in London. Its wooden beams are exposed so you are always aware that it is 'old', yet it offers every modern amenity, from full air-conditioning to an endless supply of hot water, all blended into the traditional design.

The salon has a 270-degree view of the outside and looks out onto the spacious teak deck, regularly washed down to keep it, and your feet, cool. With its banquette seating, intimate dining area and plasma screen for you to watch your adventures, this is the perfect retreat in case the weather ever turns against you. Most of the time you are either dining on the forward deck, or gazing onto the skyline of Komodo from the relaxing vantage point of the stern's cushion-strewn dais.

You sleep below deck in one of five cabins, named after some of the islands that make up the Indonesian archipelago: Borneo, Bali, Java,

at a glance

Airport	Denpasar
Airlines	Garuda, Japan Airlines, Malaysian Airlines, Qantas, Singapore Airlines, Thai Airways
Transfer time	3 mins from Amanwana by boat
Cabins	5 (all air-conditioned)
Staff ratio	2
Activities	Walking, island visits
Services	Massage
Children	All ages
Power type	2-pin round
Currency	Indonesian rupiah, US dollar
GMT	+8
Telephone	+62 371 22233
Website	www.amanresorts.com
Booking	www.diveinstyle.com

Asmat and Sumba. All are spacious and equally comfortable, with elegant interiors, full double beds, beautifully fitted shower rooms and good reading lights. The only thing to bear in mind is that Bali, probably the most attractive room, is closest to the generator.

The service and the food are the final flourishes. You are hardly aware of the boat's crew of sixteen locals, who genuinely seem to take pleasure in helping you enjoy yourself to the max. As for the food, much like Amanwana, you have a daily choice of a local or Western starter and main course, followed by an indulgent dessert.

An overnight run from Amanwana brings you directly to the heart of the Komodo National Park, not unlike *The Lost World*. The choice is then yours whether to dive, snorkel or explore. A trip to the island of Komodo is a must. This is one of only two places in the world were you will see the extraordinary Komodo dragons, 11ft-plus predators whose deadly bacterial saliva has a one hundred per cent kill rate. There is something very special about seeing them in their natural habitat, with only a ranger and a 6ft-long stick to come between you; a German baron is said to have vanished, leaving only his camera.

The *Silolona* is truly a floating Aman, a seamless extension of Amanwana. She departs from Moyo, and the standard trip is five nights; there is a package that includes two nights at the resort and she is also available for private charter. Nonetheless, even a week won't really be enough on such a boat or in such a location. It's simply fabulous, even before you get into the water – and that's where the best part awaits.

ABOVE
Manta ray are a common visitor in the waters around Komodo. Even warm-water killer whales have been spotted here.

Komodo National Park has some of the best diving in the world, with over 1,200 species of fish and 250 types of coral – and new ones are still being discovered. The sheer biodiversity is amazing and virtually anything can be found in these waters, from the rare mimic octopus to warm-water killer whales. The quantity of marine life is staggering, and much of it is remarkably unafraid of divers.

DIVING

Komodo is both a national park and a national marine park, and its status is enforced despite the locals' fondness for dynamite fishing, so the reefs are truly flourishing. Some are covered in acres of immaculate staghorns; blizzards of fish rise and fall in time with your air bubbles, while inquisitive turtles seek you out.

The marine park has two very different areas, north and south, and the *Silolona* cruises both, depending on the season. The north provides warm-water diving, with endless visibility and clear turquoise waters. As you sail south, in a matter of a few miles, the water temperature drops from a balmy 30°C (86°F) to a numbing 19°C (66°F), and swells of plankton create a drop in visibility. Komodo is where the Indian and Pacific Oceans meet, and it is this constant welling-up of cold, nutrient-rich waters, especially from the Antarctic, that brings such a variety of life. It is crucial that you are accompanied by a highly experienced guide as the strong currents can be dangerous. The *Silolona*'s instructors more than qualify.

Two dives deserve special mention, and provided your timing is right, they simply have to be experienced. The first is Tatawa Besar, a pristine, seemingly endless reef festooned with both hard and soft corals, and fronted by a small white-sand beach that is perfect for

at a glance

Level	Easy to advanced (experience required for some of the best dives)
Visibility	100ft+
Must-dives	Tatawa Besar, Tatawa Kecil, Gili Lawa Laut, Cannibal Rock, Ikelite Reef, Highway to Heaven, Castle Rock
Snorkelling	Superb
Wetsuits	3mm in north, 5mm in south
Coral	Superb
Marine life	Frogfish, leaf fish, nudibranchs, manta ray, whale shark, grey reef shark, schooling trevally, ghost pipefish, pygmy seahorse, killer whale, bumphead parrotfish, bobtail squid, mimic octopus
Other	Night dives, marine park, hyperbaric chamber in Bali (2 hrs)

OPPOSITE, CLOCKWISE FROM TOP LEFT
Anemones come in a multitude of vibrant colours; attention shell collectors – cowries are more lovely alive than dead, when their beautiful mantle enfolds their shell; a delicate porcelain crab, protected by a covering of mucus from the poisonous tentacles of an anemone; clownfish enjoy a symbiotic relationship with anemones, attracting food for their host and feeding on the leftovers.

OPPOSITE, CLOCKWISE FROM TOP LEFT
A leaf scorpionfish can only really be seen with a flashlight; lionfish float gently on the reef's edge and yet can move with incredible speed when feeding; Komodo's thriving reefs are home to shark, dolphin, whale, dugong and turtles; Komodo National Park is only accessible by boat, so there is little risk of over-diving and the sea life is quite tame.

RIGHT
Komodo is a World Heritage site and enjoys protection from overfishing and dynamiting. Its reefs, among the healthiest in Indonesia, are getting better every day.

BELOW RIGHT
Take a closer look: it may seem like there is just one frogfish in this image, but there are actually two.

lunch afterwards. Be sure to take a flashlight to bring out the amazing colours, particularly of the soft corals. There is so much to see that there is no point listing what you can expect to find.

The second dive is Tatawa Kecil, and while there are no colourful soft corals, it does reward you with blizzards of small fish exploding and retreating out of fields of staghorn. There are also bigger species including manta ray; look out for the rarer, even more striking black manta ray, which sometimes feed here. While the plankton means that visibility is far from perfect, it is this that brings in life as diverse as tuna, wahoo, bumphead parrotfish, giant wrasse, whale shark and shark. Another reason for the plethora of activity is that this small pinnacle is swept by fast currents, and currents bring predators. One end of the site is swept by powerful forces, but the other can be dived with relative ease; when the current becomes noticeable, you simply reverse the dive. Once again, your instructor's skill is essential, as without it some of these dives would be dangerous.

Komodo's underwater seascape is absolutely stunning, offering outstanding variety. It may be one of the planet's most sought-after dive destinations, but you don't have to be a diver to enjoy it. Snorkellers will be spoilt with some of the best sites in Indonesia, while those who stay above water will have an equally amazing time. There is truly something for everyone, from tranquil bays for snorkellers to mask-wrenching drift dives for seasoned thrill-seekers, from spine-tingling encounters with Komodo dragons to lazy days ending in beautiful sunsets. To be able to experience all this from such a unique and stylish boat makes it hard to beat. It's the ultimate way to visit this lost world.

diving facts and figures

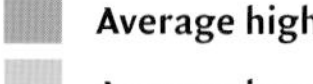

- Average high
- Average low
- Water temperature
- Rainfall

australia

Seasons are the reverse of the northern hemisphere – summer is winter and winter, summer. The figures below are for Cairns, and Lizard Island is normally drier. Don't go here especially to see whales or mantas as they are unreliable; just go, as the coral is still incredible.

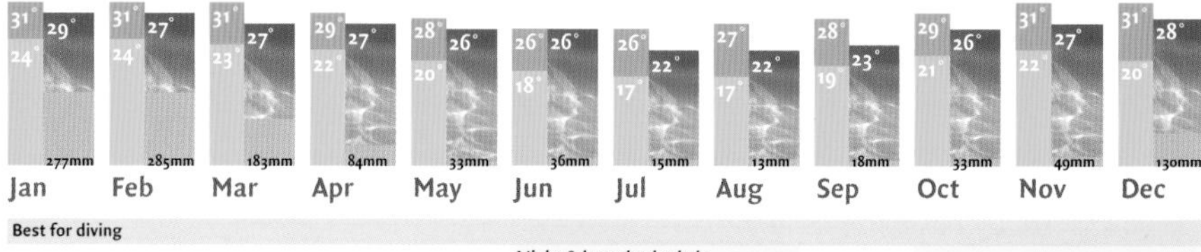

Best for diving

Minke & humpback whale

Manta

fiji

Being south of the Equator, the seasons are the reverse of the northern hemisphere, and December to April is the rainy season. The rainfall figures are for the mainland; the outlying islands, such as Vatulele, receive less rain.

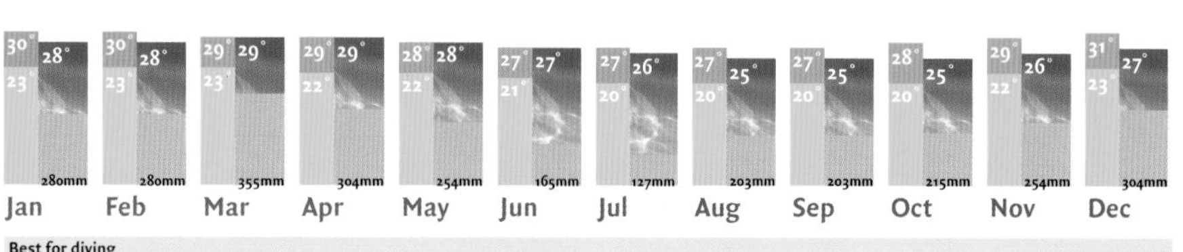

Best for diving

hawaii

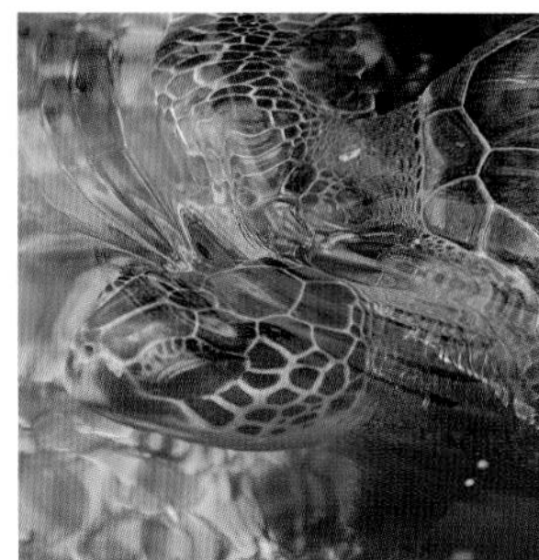

Visibility is best during the summer months, and the sea more settled, although during the winter you dive to the constant song of the humpback whale.

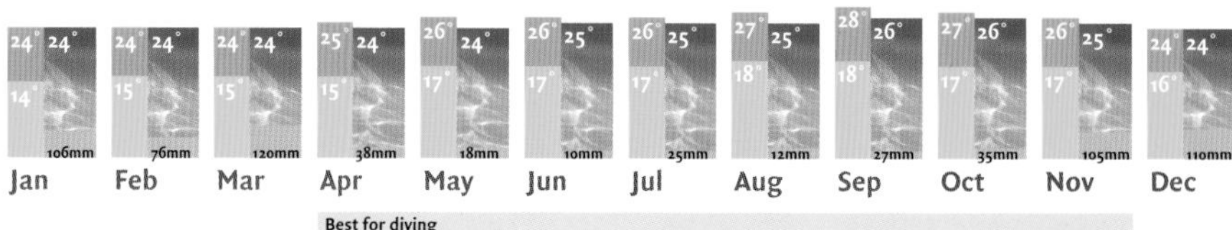

Best for diving

Manta

Dolphin

Humpback whale

french polynesia

Forget celebrating Christmas here if you want sunshine. These islands are beautiful and lush for a reason. The figures are for Bora Bora and the Society Islands; Tikehau does have less rain.

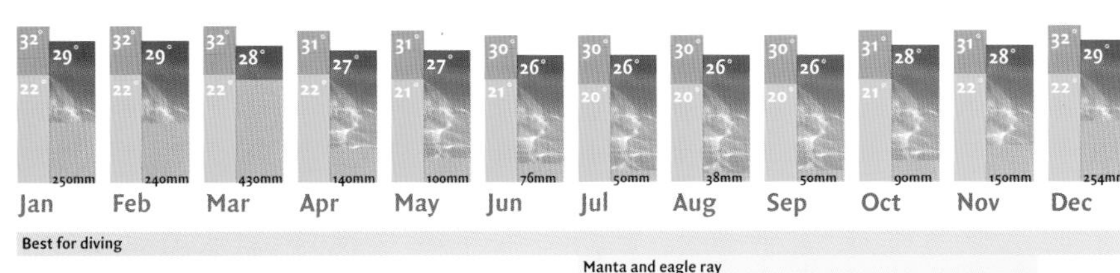

Best for diving

Manta and eagle ray

Hammerhead (Tikehau only)

Humpback whale

costa rica

May to November is rainy season (normally sunny in the morning and some rain in the afternoon) but the seas are calm, and it is the best time for the Catalina and Bat Islands. The best visibility is in the dry season, December through April.

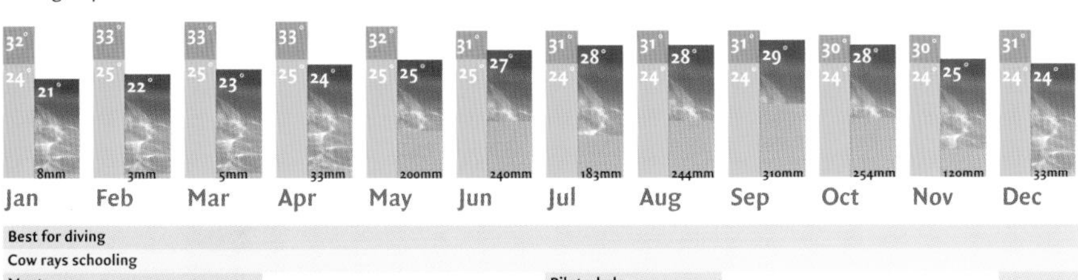

Best for diving

Cow rays schooling

Manta

Pilot whale

Whale shark

Humpback whale

Killer whale

mexico

While the weather is normally settled, remember that August to November is hurricane season. Although this is unlikely to disrupt your holiday, it should be borne in mind.

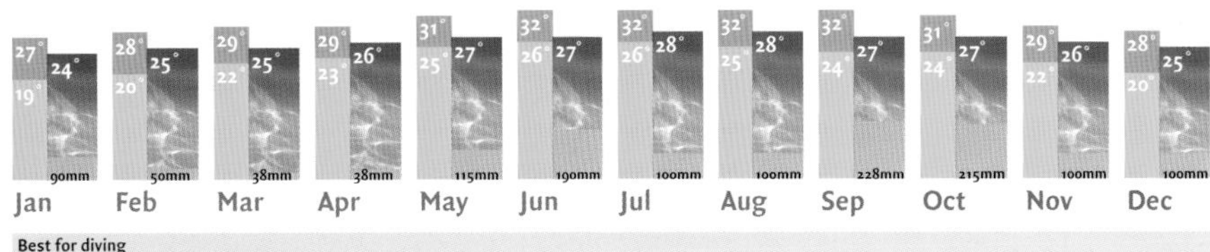

Best for diving

Whale shark

usa

Beware the almost traditional Florida 'cold snap' around the New Year.

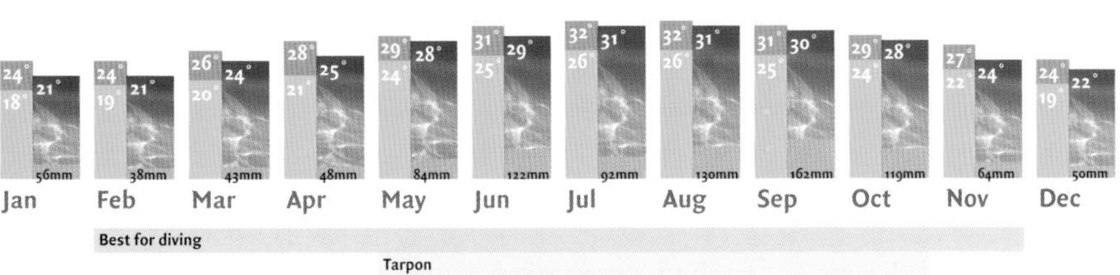

Best for diving

Tarpon

belize

This subtropical climate has a mean humidity of 83 per cent but is usually comfortable thanks to the cooling winds. Diving is great all year round, but for a guaranteed thrill, whale shark season cannot be beaten for divers and snorkellers alike.

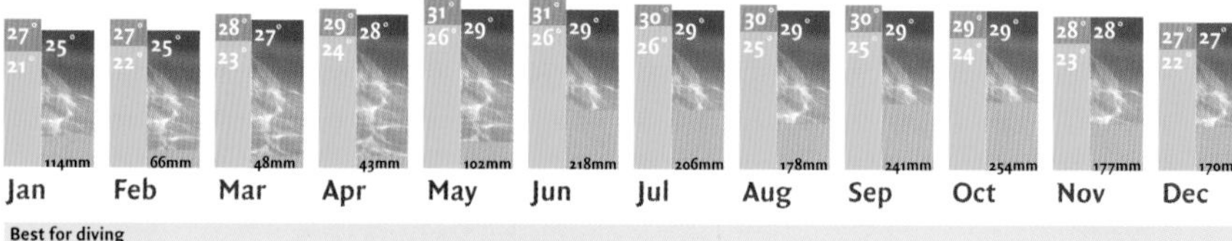

Best for diving
Grouper spawning
Whale shark
Loggerhead turtle
Manta (Glovers Reef)
Mating manatees

caribbean

August and September can be hot and still as it is hurricane season. If you're whale-watching on the *Aggressor*, take a fleece and a lightweight waterproof jacket, and note that the last trip ends at Grand Turk, a short hop from Amanyara in the Turks and Caicos, which has great diving.

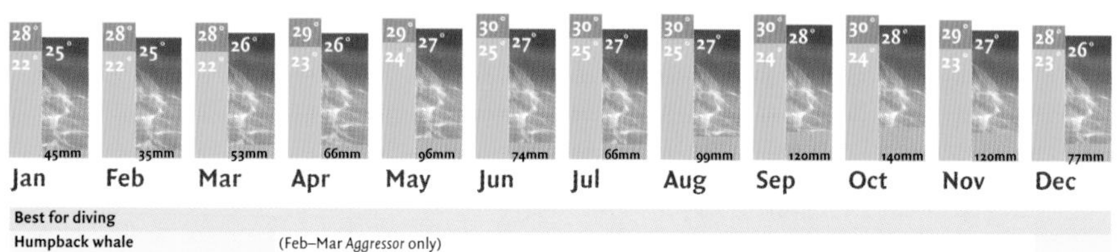

Best for diving
Humpback whale (Feb–Mar *Aggressor* only)
Tarpon and jack schools

italy

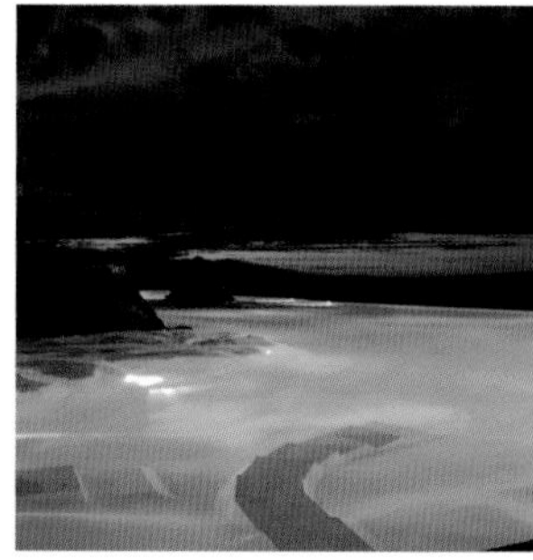

The busy season runs from 25 June to 28 August, so book early. September offers the best compromise: the waters are warm and the August rush is over.

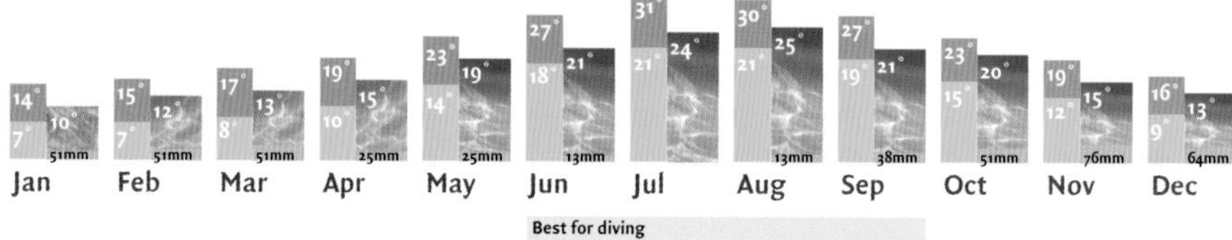

Best for diving

egypt

If you want guaranteed sunshine, just look at the rainfall figures! It gets hot in summer but if you can bear it, this is when the fish and shark form huge schools and the diving is at its zenith.

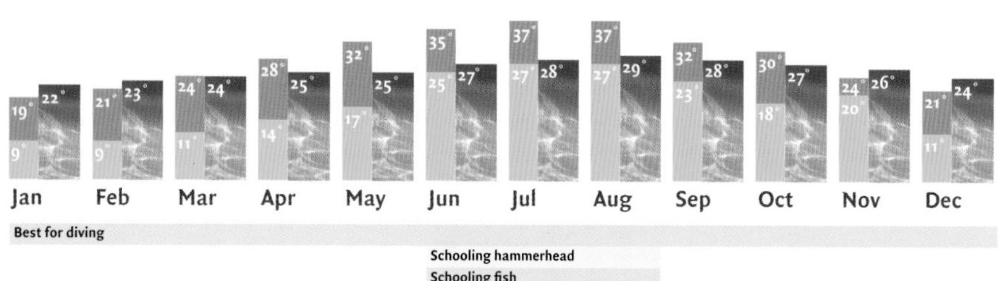

Best for diving
Schooling hammerhead
Schooling fish
Silky shark

tanzania

Late March to late May is the long rainy season and considered winter. Check the tides with the resort before you book.

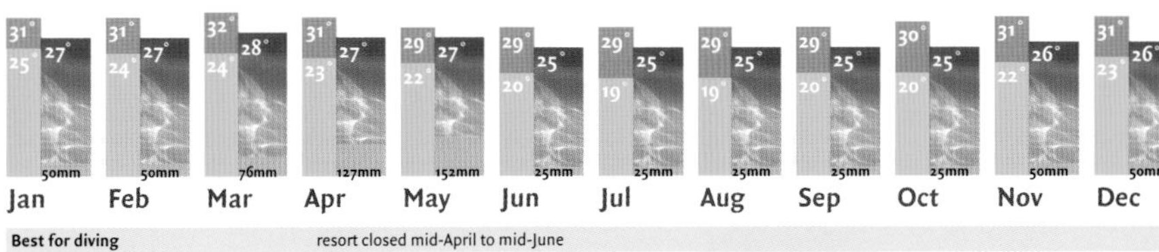

Humpback whale

Turtle hatching

mozambique

Avoid February and March when the rain can last for days at a time. If going to Marlin, book one of the newer rooms. Quilálea, meanwhile, has a great-value dive package and the best diving is on the neap tide. Manta and whale shark are only found at Marlin; Quilálea has turtles and humpback whales.

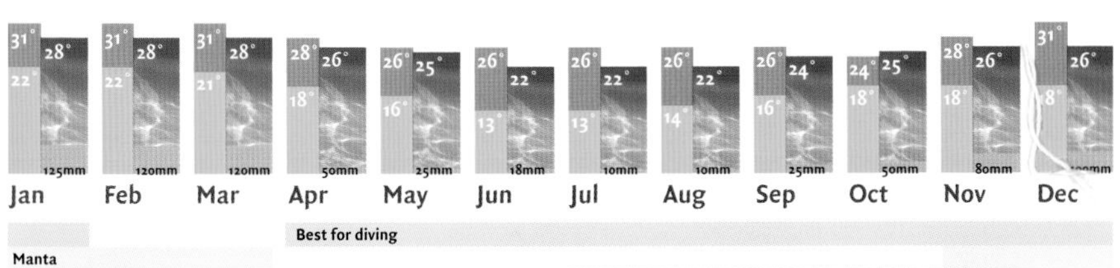

Manta

Whale shark

Humpback whales

Green turtle laying eggs

seychelles

Being close to the Equator, air and water temperatures vary little. The more humid rainy season runs from November to April, and the downpours, when they come, can be heavy, but last only a short while before the sunshine returns. Avoid July and August for diving. For whale shark, it's best to stay on Male.

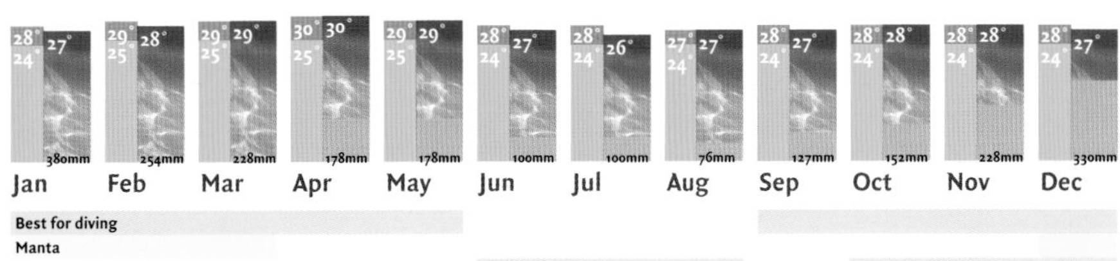

Best for diving

Manta

Whale shark

maldives

There are two seasons: the wet season from May to November, which brings mantas but has worse visibility, and the dry season from December to April, when visibility is much better (best for photos), the currents stronger, and there are more shark and eagle ray. Low season is still good weather and great diving.

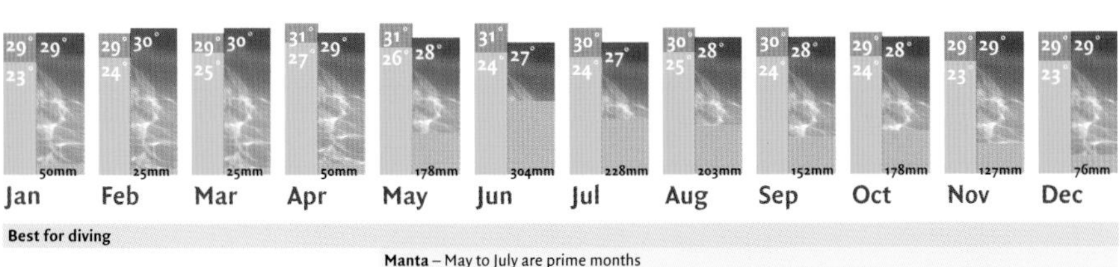

Best for diving

Manta – May to July are prime months

Whale shark

thailand

Avoid the turn of the seasons in October and May. If you especially want to dive the Similans, November to April is the time to do it as they are closed the rest of the year. For the best visibility, try and avoid the new moon; half-moon diving is best. If you're looking for whale shark and manta then head to Hin Deang and Hin Muang – a long day trip.

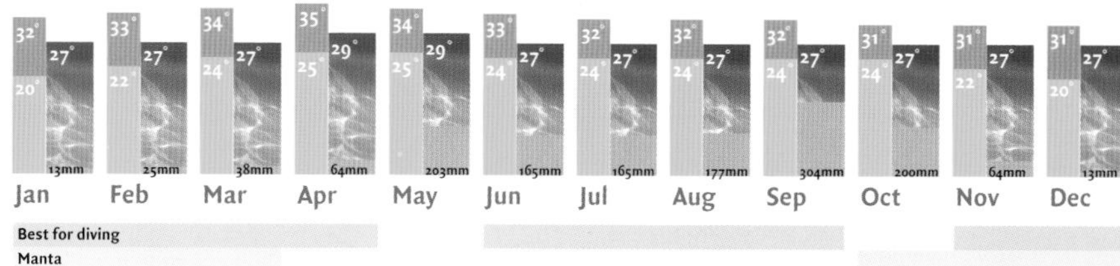

philippines

The best and calmest conditions are from March to May, when you can dive most sites, although it is good all year round with at least one of Pamalican's coasts always being accessible to dive.

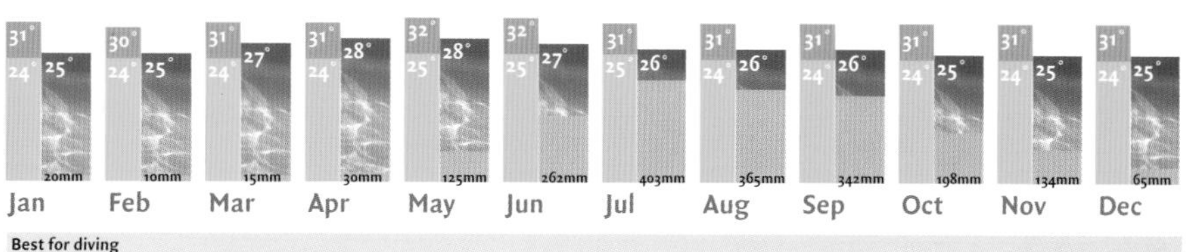

palau

May to November is not so good due to rougher weather, so you may not get to dive Blue Corner. April to June is less suitable for novice divers. Make sure you book a new room.

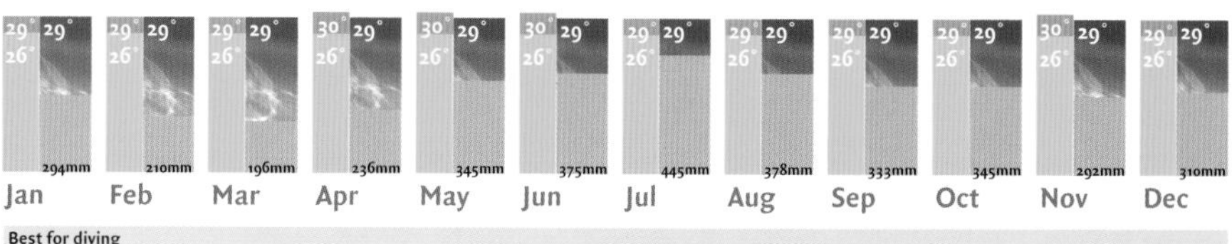

indonesia

Avoid the rainy season between January and March. Diving is always fantastic but it is at its very best between April and October. The figures are for Moyo and north Komodo, whereas the water can be up to 8 degrees colder in south Komodo.

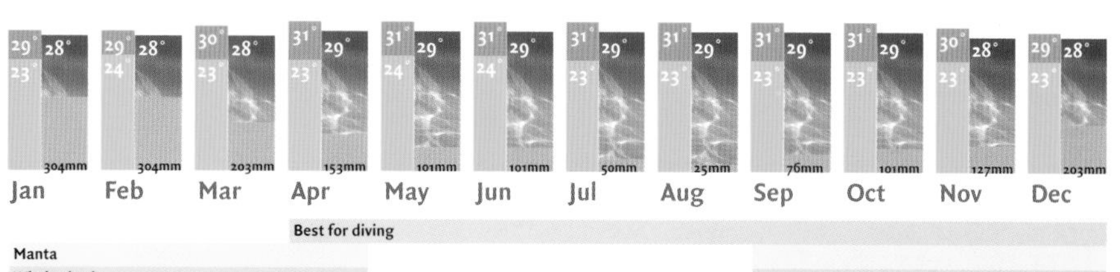